P9-DWK-430

Stews

GENERAL EDITOR
CHUCK WILLIAMS

RECIPES
LORA BRODY

PHOTOGRAPHY
ALLAN ROSENBERG

TIME
LIFE
BOOKS

Time-Life Books is a division of
TIME LIFE INCORPORATED

President and CEO: John M. Fahey, Jr.
President, Time-Life Books: John D. Hall

TIME-LIFE CUSTOM PUBLISHING

Vice President and Publisher: Terry Newell
Sales Director: Frances C. Mangan
Editorial Director: Donia Steele

WILLIAMS-SONOMA
Founder/Vice-Chairman: Chuck Williams

WELDON OWEN INC.
President: John Owen
Publisher/Vice President: Wendely Harvey
Associate Publisher: Laurie Wertz
Managing Editor: Lisa Chaney Atwood
Consulting Editor: Norman Kolpas
Copy Editor: Sharon Silva
Design: John Bull, The Book Design Company
Production Director: Stephanie Sherman
Production Editor: Janique Gascoigne
Co-Editions Director: Derek Barton
Co-Editions Production Manager (US): Tarji Mickelson
Food Photographer: Allan Rosenberg
Additional Food Photography: Allen V. Lott
Primary Food & Prop Stylist: Sandra Griswold
Food Stylist: Heidi Gintner
Food Stylist Assistant: Nette Scott
Food & Prop Assistant: Elizabeth C. Davis
Glossary Illustrations: Alice Harth

The Williams-Sonoma Kitchen Library
conceived and produced by Weldon Owen Inc.
814 Montgomery St., San Francisco, CA 94133

In collaboration with Williams-Sonoma
100 North Point, San Francisco, CA 94133

Production by Mandarin Offset, Hong Kong
Printed in China

A Note on Weights and Measures:
All recipes include customary U.S. and metric
measurements. Metric conversions are based on
a standard developed for these books and have
been rounded off. Actual weights may vary.

A Weldon Owen Production

Copyright © 1995 Weldon Owen Inc.
All rights reserved, including the right of
reproduction in whole or in part in any form.

Library of Congress
Cataloging-in-Publication Data:

Brody, Lora.
    Stews / general editor, Chuck Williams ; recipes, Lora Brody ;
photography, Allan Rosenberg.
        p.   cm. — (Williams-Sonoma kitchen library)
    Includes index.
    ISBN 0-7835-0307-5
    1. Stews.   I. Title.   II. Series.
TX693.W56   1995
641.8'23—dc20   94-48065
                                                    CIP

Contents

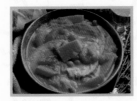

POULTRY 15

MEAT 41

SEAFOOD 73

VEGETABLES 93

INTRODUCTION

A stew is among the easiest dishes to prepare. You generally don't have to be precise about measuring or cutting up the ingredients, and you can put them all into a pot within a matter of minutes. Then you can leave the stew alone to simmer while you do something else.

Serving a stew is equally straightforward. Just ladle it onto plates or into bowls and accompany it with a salad, some good bread and a simple dessert. If the pot the stew was cooked in is attractive, you can place it right on the table and let guests help themselves. Whether you're feeding family or friends, a stew is a meal that everyone will enjoy.

This volume showcases a diverse collection of stews that bring with them all of these attributes. There are braises in these pages, too, which differ from stews only in that they are generally larger pieces of food cooked in less liquid. The eight pages that follow cover all the basics you need to know for making these easy main courses. They are followed by 45 stew and braise recipes, divided into chapters by main ingredients: poultry, meat, seafood and vegetables.

As you look through these recipes, you'll also discover another benefit of stews: Many make use of tough, less costly cuts of meat that are full of flavor and reach absolute tenderness through slow, gentle simmering. Yet one more reason to take the smart, easy approach to good cooking by preparing simple and delicious stews.

Chuck Williams

EQUIPMENT

Good, sturdy cooking vessels and a collection of basic tools ensure perfect results for stewing

The equipment essential for stewing is basic: a sturdy, good-capacity pot or stove-top casserole to hold main ingredients, liquids and seasonings during their long, slow simmering.

All the other items shown here, most of which are part of any well-stocked kitchen, merely make the job of cooking a stew even more efficient. Good, sharp knives, for example, ease the task of cutting meat, poultry, seafood or vegetables into uniform pieces that will cook easily, and of carving large stewed cuts of meat into individual servings. A full complement of basic tools—including wooden and metal spoons—assist in simple tasks such as deglazing and skimming (see pages 10–11).

1. Sauté Pan
For browning of ingredients in the early stages of stewing or braising, select a good-quality heavy metal pan large enough to hold ingredients in a single layer without crowding. Straight sides about 2½ inches (6 cm) high help contain splattering. If the pan is to be used for the moist cooking stage as well, a close-fitting lid helps contain moisture.

2. Baking Sheet
Flat and resilient sheet of regular or nonstick aluminum for toasting nuts and general baking purposes.

3. Pot Holder
Heavy-duty cotton provides good protection from hot cookware.

4. Saucepan
For precooking vegetables and preparing sauces.

5. Stockpot
Tall, large-capacity pot with close-fitting lid, for cooking bulky ingredients and making stock or large quantities of stew. Select a good-quality, heavy-bottomed pot that absorbs and transfers heat well. Enameled steel, shown here, or anodized aluminum cleans easily.

6. Cutting Board
Acrylic boards are tough, resilient, nonporous and easy to clean. Be sure to wash thoroughly after every use.

7. Chef's Knife
All-purpose knife for chopping and slicing vegetables, large items or large quantities of ingredients.

8. Carving Knife
Long, sturdy but flexible blade easily slices through large cuts of meat or poultry for serving.

9. Carving Fork
Sturdy two-pronged fork steadies meats during carving.

10. Paring Knife
For peeling vegetables and cutting up small ingredients.

11. Assorted Kitchen Tools and Spoons
Crockery jar holds slotted spoon for transferring small ingredients without their cooking liquid; fine-mesh sieve for straining stocks and cooking liquids; metal spoon for skimming off fat or for serving stews; wooden spoon and spatula for stirring and deglazing; ladle for serving stews; metal tongs for transferring large ingredients from one cooking vessel to another; and wire whisk for stirring together flour and fat to thicken sauces.

12. Baking Dish
Large rectangular porcelain baking dish for oven-baked stews, usually covered with aluminum foil.

13. Stew Pot
For use on the stove top or in the oven, large-capacity enameled metal cooking vessel with a heavy bottom and tight-fitting ovenproof lid.

14. Mixing Bowls
Sturdy bowls in a wide range of sizes for holding cut-up ingredients, seasonings and liquids before cooking; for presoaking dried beans; and for mixing stuffings or dumpling dough.

15. Frying Pan
Choose good-quality, heavy stainless steel, aluminum, cast iron or enamel for rapid, efficient browning and sautéing. Sloped shallow sides allow moisture to evaporate quickly so ingredients fry rather than steam cook.

16. Measuring Cups and Spoons
For accurate measuring of liquid ingredients, choose heavy-duty, heat-resistant glass cups, marked on one side in cups and ounces and on the other in milliliters; lip and handle allow for easy pouring. For accurate measuring of dry ingredients, choose good-quality calibrated metal or plastic cups and spoons in graduated sizes, with straight rims that allow for leveling.

17. Steamer Insert
Anodized aluminum, stainless-steel or enameled metal steamer insert fits snugly in a pan filled with simmering liquid, for steaming dumplings to garnish stews. A stainless-steel steamer rack, most of which adjust easily to fit pans of varying sizes, may also be used.

MAKING STOCKS

Made from the slow simmering of fish, poultry, meat or vegetables in water, stock is often the fundamental cooking liquid of stews.

Although good-quality canned or frozen stocks or reconstituted stock concentrates may be used for any of the recipes in this book, they are often saltier than homemade varieties and will require an adjustment of seasoning in most recipes for which they are used.

Vegetable Stock

Homemade vegetable stock offers a more flavorful and economical alternative to the canned or concentrated varieties. Sautéing the vegetables before adding water gives this particular stock a special depth of flavor.

2 tablespoons vegetable oil
2 large sweet onions, coarsely chopped
4 celery stalks with leaves, coarsely chopped
3 carrots, peeled and coarsely chopped
1 green bell pepper (capsicum), seeded, deribbed and coarsely chopped
10 cups (2½ qt/2.5 l) water
1 teaspoon salt
bouquet garni *(recipe on page 10)*

*I*n a large stockpot over medium heat, warm the vegetable oil. Add the onions, celery, carrots and bell pepper and sauté, stirring, until the onions are translucent, about 10 minutes. Add the water, salt and bouquet garni; bring to a gentle boil. Boil gently, uncovered, for 30 minutes.

Remove from the heat and strain through a fine-mesh sieve lined with cheesecloth (muslin) into a clean container. Use immediately, or cover and refrigerate for up to 5 days or freeze for up to 1 year.

Makes about 8 cups (64 fl oz/2 l)

Fish Stock

For a quick substitute to homemade fish stock, use good-quality bottled, canned or frozen fish stock; or dissolve 1 fish bouillon cube in 1 cup (8 fl oz/250 ml) hot water for each cup of fish stock that is required. Since commercial fish stock base can be quite salty, adjust the seasoning in each recipe as necessary.

2 tablespoons olive oil
2 yellow onions, coarsely chopped
1 large leek, white part only, carefully washed and coarsely chopped
3 celery stalks with leaves, coarsely chopped
1½ lb (750 g) white fish fillets, such as cod, flounder or sole
8 cups (64 fl oz/2 l) water
bouquet garni *(recipe on page 10)*
½ teaspoon salt, optional

*I*n a large stockpot over medium heat, warm the olive oil. Add the onions, leek and celery and sauté, stirring, until slightly tender but not quite translucent, about 5 minutes. Add the fish and sauté, stirring, for 5 minutes longer. Pour in the water and add the bouquet garni and the salt, if desired. Bring to a simmer, then reduce the heat to low, cover and simmer gently for 20 minutes. Do not allow the stock to boil.

Remove from the heat and strain through a fine-mesh sieve lined with cheesecloth (muslin) into a clean container. Reserve the fish fillets for another use, if desired. Use immediately, or cover and refrigerate overnight or freeze for up to 6 months.

Makes 6–7 cups (48–56 fl oz/1.5–1.75 l)

Chicken Stock

Any type of chicken can be used for making this stock, although pieces of a stewing chicken (usually a more mature bird) will yield the most flavor. Cooking the meat with skin and fat attached is another flavor booster.

2½ lb (1.25 kg) chicken pieces, including bones
8 cups (64 fl oz/2 l) water
4 celery stalks with leaves, coarsely chopped
2 carrots, peeled and coarsely chopped
2 yellow onions, coarsely chopped
2 leeks, white part only, carefully washed and
    coarsely chopped
bouquet garni *(recipe on page 10)*
½ teaspoon salt

*I*n a large stockpot over medium-high heat, combine the chicken and water. Bring to a gentle boil and boil for 30 minutes. Using a large spoon, skim off any scum that forms on the surface.

  Add the celery, carrots, onions, leeks, bouquet garni and salt. Cover partially and boil gently for 30 minutes longer; check periodically, skimming off any scum that may form on the surface.

  Remove from the heat. Using a slotted spoon, remove the chicken pieces and reserve for another use, if desired. Strain the stock through a fine-mesh sieve lined with cheesecloth (muslin) into a clean container. Let cool briefly, then refrigerate until the fat solidifies on the surface. Using a slotted spoon, lift off the fat and discard. Use immediately, or cover and refrigerate for up to 5 days or freeze for up to 6 months.

Makes about 5 cups (40 fl oz/1.25 l)

Beef Stock

Although most beef stocks are made with a combination of beef bones and meat, this short-cut recipe, which uses only meat, yields a delicious result. Good-quality purchased beef stock can be used in any recipe calling for beef stock.

2 tablespoons olive oil
1 lb (500 g) beef stew meat, cut into 1-inch
    (2.5-cm) cubes
1 large sweet onion, cut in half and then into
    slices ¼ inch (6 mm) thick
8 cups (64 fl oz/2 l) hot water
3 celery stalks with leaves, coarsely chopped
2 carrots, peeled and coarsely chopped
bouquet garni *(recipe on page 10)*

*I*n a large stockpot over medium-high heat, warm the olive oil. Add the beef cubes and brown well on all sides, 3–4 minutes. Add the onion and sauté, stirring, until the browned bits from the pot bottom begin to cling to the slices and the onion is dark brown but not blackened, about 8 minutes. Stir in 2–3 tablespoons of the hot water if necessary to keep the onions from sticking.

  Add the remaining hot water, celery, carrots and bouquet garni and bring to a simmer. Cover partially and simmer over medium-low heat for 1 hour.

  Remove from the heat and strain the stock through a fine-mesh sieve lined with cheesecloth (muslin) into a clean container. Remove the meat and reserve for another use, if desired. Let the stock cool briefly, then refrigerate until the fat solidifies on the surface. Using a slotted spoon, lift off the fat and discard. Use immediately, or cover and refrigerate for up to 5 days or freeze for up to 6 months.

Makes 6–7 cups (48–56 fl oz/1.5–1.75 l)

Stewing Basics

The cooking technique known as stewing may be explained in one easy step: Combine solids and liquids and simmer until done.

A few more simple steps, however, guarantee results as delicious and tender as possible. Browning main ingredients in advance helps seal in their juices, and deglazing the pan after browning adds extra flavor. Attention to seasonings, as in the bouquet garni (below), further contributes to the taste of the finished dish. Safeguard tenderness with careful simmering and knowing how to test meat for doneness.

If you like, you can remove any additional fat from the stew, both during and after cooking, to ensure that it will have a pure taste and will be healthful and easy to digest.

Making a Bouquet Garni

This combination of herbs and spices enhances a variety of stews. Add it to the stews as they simmer, then discard before serving.

6 whole peppercorns
1 bay leaf
1 clove garlic, sliced
3 fresh parsley sprigs

Cut a 6-inch (15-cm) square of cheesecloth (muslin). Place the peppercorns, bay leaf, garlic and parsley sprigs on the center of the cheesecloth, bring the corners together and tie securely with kitchen string. Alternatively, combine all the ingredients in a tea ball and secure the top in place. Use as directed in individual recipes.

Browning

Most meat and poultry stew recipes call for the main ingredient to be browned. Use a large cooking vessel wide enough to hold the meat or poultry in a single layer without crowding, thus allowing moisture to escape without hindering the browning process.

Browning the meat.
In a sauté pan or frying pan, heat a thin film of fat or oil. Taking care not to crowd the pan, and working in batches if necessary, add the meat—here, pork—and turn until evenly browned on all sides.

Deglazing

When ingredients have been browned before stewing, the flavorful glaze of juices that forms on the bottom of the pan can provide a rich source of extra flavor. Deglazing—dissolving the glaze with some liquid—enables you to capture that flavor for the stew.

Deglazing the pan.
After the meat has browned, remove it from the pan. Add to the pan the deglazing liquid called for in the recipe. Over heat, stir and scrape vigorously with a wooden spoon to dislodge any browned bits from the pan bottom and dissolve the glazed juices.

SIMMERING

If a stew is allowed to boil for any length of time, the intense heat can toughen meat or poultry or disintegrate delicate seafood. A carefully regulated bare simmer, on the other hand, gently coaxes the main ingredients to tenderness.

Simmering a stew.
Following the recipe instructions, put the solid and liquid ingredients and seasonings into a pot or casserole and bring the liquid to a boil. Reduce the heat to maintain a bare but steady simmer, so that bubbles rise to the surface of the stew but do not break, and then cover the vessel if specified in the recipe.

TESTING MEAT FOR DONENESS

A stew is judged done at the point at which its featured ingredient is absolutely tender. In most cases, doneness can be tested simply with a long-handled fork. Start checking at the earliest time specified in the recipe.

Piercing the meat.
Cook the stew for the minimum time called for in the recipe. Then, use a fork to test the main ingredient for doneness: It should be tender enough to yield gently when pierced; if not, continue cooking about 10 minutes longer before testing again.

REMOVING THE FAT

Stewing offers two opportunities to eliminate fat. Much of the fat in meat or poultry will rise to the surface during simmering, at which point it can be skimmed off. If the finished stew is refrigerated, the fat will solidify on top, where it can be easily lifted off.

Skimming off fat.
As the stew or stock slowly reaches a simmer, use a large, shallow spoon to skim off pools of fat that rise to the surface (shown here on chicken stock); also remove any frothy scum from the surface. After a simmer has been reached, continue to skim off fat and scum from time to time.

Removing solidified fat.
If a stew or stock has been refrigerated overnight or longer, use a metal spoon that is slotted or solid depending on the amount of fat, and lift off the fat from the surface before reheating.

THICKENING A STEW

Many stews thicken naturally during cooking, as their liquids reduce or as starchy vegetables such as beans or potatoes contribute their own body. Other recipes, however, sometimes call for the addition of a flour-and-butter roux or cornstarch (cornflour) to thicken the stew liquid.

MAKING A ROUX

For the best results when thickening stewing liquids with a flour-and-butter roux, allow sufficient simmering time to eliminate the raw taste of the flour.

Melt butter in a saucepan or pot over medium heat and, whisking constantly, sprinkle in flour. Continue whisking for 2–3 minutes. Slowly pour in liquid, whisking continuously to avoid lumps; then cook, stirring, until smooth and thickened.

ADDING CORNSTARCH

To avoid the formation of lumps, dissolve cornstarch completely in a little cold liquid before adding it to the stew.

In a cup or small bowl, stir cornstarch together with just enough cold liquid to dissolve it completely. Then, stirring the stew continuously, slowly pour in the cornstarch mixture. Continue simmering until the liquid thickens.

STEW ACCOMPANIMENTS

Although a stew is, almost by definition, a one-dish meal, many traditional recipes call for an added starchy accompaniment such as dumplings (see recipe, right), boiled or mashed potatoes, steamed rice, or cooked pasta or noodles.

Potatoes may be easily cooked by peeling them, cutting them into 2-inch (5-cm) pieces and then boiling them in a large quantity of lightly salted water until tender when pierced with a fork, about 15 minutes. Use any type of potato you like. Drain the cooked pieces well, then toss them with a little butter and season to taste with salt and white pepper. Or pass them through a potato ricer or a food mill or mash them with a potato masher and then mix them with some butter, warmed half-and-half (half cream) and with salt and white pepper to taste.

The cooking time for rice and the proportions of water to rice depend upon the variety you select. Follow package directions carefully. Follow them, too, for noodles or other pasta, taking care to use enough water to let them circulate freely during cooking; they're cooked perfectly when an individual piece removed from the pot is *al dente*— tender but firm.

Old-fashioned Dumplings

These light and airy dumplings effectively capture the essence of a stew by soaking up the juices into their soft interiors. Directions are provided here for cooking the dumplings directly on top of a stew and for steaming on a plate in a steamer. The latter method is necessary when the stew includes ingredients that are too delicate for the low boil required to cook the dumplings.

2 cups (10 oz/315 g) all-purpose (plain) flour
2 teaspoons baking powder
¼ teaspoon baking soda (bicarbonate of soda)
½ teaspoon salt
1 egg, beaten
¾ cup (6 fl oz/180 ml) milk

In a bowl, sift together the flour, baking powder, baking soda and salt. Add the egg and milk and mix with a fork until the flour is absorbed.

Bring the stew to a gentle boil.

To cook the dumplings on top of the stew, dip a large metal spoon into cold water, then scoop out a spoonful of the moist dumpling dough and drop it on top of the stew. Repeat with the remaining dough. Try to have the dumplings rest on something solid in the stew; do not allow them to float in the liquid. If there is too much liquid for the dumplings to rest on solid ingredients, re-move as much of the liquid as necessary and return it to the stew before serving. Cover and cook the dumplings over medium heat until a toothpick inserted into the center of a dumpling comes out clean, about 12 minutes.

To steam the dumplings on a plate, grease a heatproof plate with vegetable oil, butter or margarine and place the plate on a rack in a steamer pan filled with water to a depth of about 1 inch (2.5 cm). Bring the water to a boil over high heat. Following the directions for form-ing the dumplings on top of a stew, drop the dumplings onto the plate. Cover the steamer and steam until the dumplings test done, about 20 minutes. Slide the dumplings on top of the stew and serve immediately.

Makes about 16 dumplings; serves 4

Cornbread Dumplings
Substitute 1 cup (5 oz/155 g) fine-grind cornmeal for 1 cup (5 oz/155 g) of the flour.

Buttermilk Dumplings
Substitute ¾ cup (6 fl oz/180 ml) buttermilk for the milk.

Cooking dumplings on top of the stew.
For each dumpling, using a large metal spoon dipped in cold water, scoop up a spoonful of dough and drop it into the stew, letting it rest on something solid. Cover and cook until a toothpick inserted into a dumpling comes out clean, about 12 minutes.

Steaming dumplings on a plate.
Grease a heatproof plate and place on a steamer insert or rack above 1 inch (2.5 cm) of boiling water. Using a large spoon dipped in cold water, scoop up spoonfuls of dough and drop them onto the plate. Cover and steam until a toothpick inserted into a dumpling comes out clean, about 20 minutes.

Apricot Turkey Stew

2 tablespoons vegetable oil

1 whole turkey breast, about 4 lb (2 kg), skinned and trimmed of fat

¼ cup (2 oz/60 g) butter or margarine

2 large sweet onions, cut in half lengthwise and then crosswise into slices ½ inch (12 mm) thick

4 large carrots, peeled and cut into 2-inch (5-cm) lengths

¾ cup (4½ oz/140 g) golden raisins (sultanas)

1 cup (6 oz/185 g) dried apricots

4 sweet potatoes, peeled and quartered

1 can (6 oz/185 g) frozen orange juice concentrate, undiluted, partially thawed

½ cup (5 oz/155 g) apricot jam

1½ cups (12 fl oz/375 ml) sweet white wine

salt and freshly ground pepper

This aromatic, slightly sweet stew is a great make-ahead meal because it tastes even better reheated. A boned, rolled turkey breast used in place of the bone-in breast simplifies the preparation. Substitute homemade chicken stock (recipe on page 9) or purchased chicken stock for the white wine, if you wish. For an extra-rich dish, spoon brimming ladlefuls of the stew over a bed of mashed potatoes.

*I*n an 8-qt (8-l) heavy-bottomed stew pot over medium-high heat, warm the vegetable oil. Add the turkey breast and brown on both sides, turning once, until golden, about 8 minutes.

Turn the turkey breast breastbone up and add the butter or margarine. When the butter or margarine melts, add the onions, carrots, raisins, apricots and sweet potatoes, mixing well. In a small bowl, stir together the orange juice concentrate, apricot jam and wine and pour into the pot. Toss the vegetables to coat them evenly with the mixture. Bring to a simmer, reduce the heat to medium-low, cover and simmer gently for 2 hours.

Turn the turkey breast over, remove the bones and continue to simmer gently, uncovered, until the turkey is tender and cooked through and the vegetables are soft, about 30 minutes longer.

Transfer the turkey breast to a cutting board and cut it across the grain into slices ½ inch (12 mm) thick. Return the slices to the pot and gently mix them into the vegetables. Heat to serving temperature and season to taste with salt and pepper.

Spoon into warmed shallow bowls and serve.

Serves 8

Moroccan Chicken

½ cup (2 oz/60 g) slivered blanched
   almonds
2 tablespoons olive oil
4 skinless, boneless chicken breast
   halves, about 1½ lb (750 g) total
   weight, cut into bite-sized pieces
2 teaspoons peeled and finely chopped
   fresh ginger
1 large sweet onion, cut into bite-sized
   pieces
3 large carrots, peeled and cut into
   1-inch (2.5-cm) pieces
1 large green bell pepper (capsicum),
   seeded, deribbed and cut lengthwise
   into strips ½ inch (12 mm) wide
2 teaspoons ground turmeric
½ cup (4 fl oz/125 ml) chicken stock
   (recipe on page 9)
⅓ cup (2 oz/60 g) pitted green olives,
   sliced
salt and freshly ground pepper

The combination of turmeric, olives and almonds gives this North African–inspired dish special character. If you like, serve it over couscous and garnish with thinly sliced lemons.

❖

Preheat an oven to 350°F (180°C). Spread the almonds on a baking sheet or in a shallow pan and bake until lightly toasted, about 5 minutes. Set aside.

In a 4-qt (4-l) heavy-bottomed stew pot over medium-high heat, warm the olive oil. Add the chicken pieces and sauté, stirring, until golden brown, 8–10 minutes. Using a slotted spoon, transfer the chicken to a dish.

Add the ginger, onion and carrots to the same pot and sauté over medium-high heat, stirring, until the onion is tender, about 5 minutes.

Return the chicken to the pot and add the bell pepper and turmeric and mix well. Add the chicken stock and, using a large spoon, deglaze the pot over medium-high heat by stirring to dislodge any browned bits on the pot bottom. Bring to a simmer. Reduce the heat to medium-low, cover and simmer gently until the chicken is tender, about 15 minutes.

Add the olives and toasted almonds and stir well. Season to taste with salt and pepper.

Spoon into warmed shallow bowls or plates and serve.

Serves 4

Chicken Breasts with Artichokes and Lemon

3 tablespoons butter or margarine
8 skinless chicken breast halves, about
  3 lb (1.5 kg) total weight
½ cup (4 fl oz/125 ml) dry white wine
1 large sweet onion, cut in half and
  then into slices ½ inch (12 mm) thick
1 package (10 oz/315 g) frozen artichoke
  hearts, thawed and cut into halves
¾ cup (6 fl oz/180 ml) chicken stock
  (recipe on page 9)
½ teaspoon dried thyme
salt and freshly ground pepper
1 lemon, thinly sliced

Here, the flavors of the Mediterranean are combined in an easily prepared stew that makes a perfect springtime meal. Serve it over orzo tossed with olive oil, thyme, lemon zest and a pinch of red pepper flakes.

*I*n a 4-qt (4-l) heavy-bottomed stew pot over medium to medium-high heat, melt 2 tablespoons of the butter or margarine. Working in batches if necessary, add the chicken breasts and brown on all sides until they are a rich gold, 8–10 minutes; do not allow the butter to become dark brown. Using a slotted spoon, transfer the breasts to a dish. Pour the wine into the pot and, using a large spoon, deglaze over medium-high heat by stirring to dislodge any browned bits from the pot bottom. Pour the liquid over the chicken. Wipe the pot clean.

  In the same pot over medium heat, melt the remaining 1 tablespoon butter or margarine. Add the onion and sauté, stirring, until translucent, about 5 minutes. Return the chicken and juices to the pot and add the artichokes, chicken stock and thyme. Stir well and bring to a simmer over medium-low heat. Cover and simmer gently until the chicken is tender and cooked through, 20–25 minutes. To test, cut into a chicken breast with a sharp knife; the meat should be opaque throughout. Season to taste with salt and pepper.

  Spoon into warmed shallow bowls, garnish with the lemon slices and serve.

Serves 6–8

19

Chinese Chicken Stew with Straw Mushrooms

2 tablespoons vegetable oil

1 stewing chicken, about 3½ lb (1.75 kg), legs and wings cut off, body skinned and quartered

1 cup (8 fl oz/250 ml) water

1 clove garlic

2 teaspoons peeled and finely chopped fresh ginger

½ cup (2½ oz/75 g) coarsely chopped yellow onion

6 green (spring) onions, including tender green tops, trimmed and cut on the diagonal into 1-inch (2.5-cm) pieces

2 tablespoons soy sauce

2 tablespoons dry sherry

1 tablespoon cornstarch (cornflour) dissolved in 2 tablespoons cold water

1 can (8 oz/250 g) straw mushrooms, drained

salt and freshly ground pepper

This dish is not only delicious, but low in fat as well. Serve with rice or bean-thread noodles and garnish with extra green onions, if you like.

In a 4-qt (4-l) heavy-bottomed stew pot over medium-high heat, warm 1 tablespoon of the vegetable oil. Add all the chicken pieces and sauté, stirring, until lightly golden, about 5 minutes. Slowly add the water, then bring to a simmer over medium heat. Cover and simmer until the meat easily separates from the bones and is opaque throughout, about 30 minutes.

Using tongs, transfer the chicken to a plate. Using a large spoon, skim off the fat from the surface of the stock. Strain the stock through a fine-mesh sieve into a clean container and set aside. When the chicken is cool enough to handle, remove the meat from the chicken quarters, then skin and bone the legs and remove as much meat as possible from the legs and wings. Cut all the meat into bite-sized pieces. Set aside.

In the same pot over medium-high heat, warm the remaining 1 tablespoon vegetable oil. Add the garlic and sauté, stirring, until golden, about 2 minutes. Discard the garlic. Add the ginger and yellow onion and sauté, stirring, until the onion is translucent, about 5 minutes. Return the chicken meat to the pot over medium-high heat, along with the green onions, soy sauce, sherry and ¾ cup (6 fl oz/180 ml) of the reserved stock. Quickly stir the cornstarch mixture and add it to the pot, stirring it in well.

Add the mushrooms and mix in gently. Cover and simmer over low heat for about 10 minutes, to blend the flavors. Season to taste with salt and pepper.

Spoon into warmed shallow bowls and serve.

Serves 4

Chicken Stuffed with Corn Bread and Sausage

1 stewing chicken, 4–5 lb (2–2.5 kg)

½ lb (250 g) bulk pork sausage meat

2 large sweet onions, cut in half and then into slices ½ inch (12 mm) thick

1 cup (8 fl oz/250 ml) chicken stock *(recipe on page 9)*

2 cups (4 oz/125 g) crumbled dried corn bread or corn bread stuffing mix

1 cup (8 fl oz/250 ml) water

2 tablespoons butter or margarine, melted

1 green bell pepper (capsicum), seeded, deribbed and coarsely chopped

3 tablespoons fresh rosemary leaves or 1 teaspoon dried rosemary

4 carrots, peeled and cut into 1½-inch (4-cm) pieces

6–8 small red new potatoes, unpeeled

salt and freshly ground pepper

Italian sausage seasoned with fennel seeds would be good in this midwinter treat. Serve with steamed fennel.

*I*f the neck and giblets have been included in the chicken cavity, reserve for another use. Pat the chicken dry with paper towels. In an 8-qt (8-l) stew pot over medium-high heat, sauté the sausage, stirring and breaking up any lumps, until browned, 3–5 minutes. Using a slotted spoon, transfer to paper towels to drain. Pour off the fat from the pot, but leave any browned bits.

Reduce the heat to medium, add the onions and sauté, stirring, until translucent, about 5 minutes. Add 2–3 tablespoons of the chicken stock if the onions begin to stick. Add the remaining stock and deglaze the pot by stirring to dislodge any browned bits on the pot bottom. Remove from the heat and set aside.

In a bowl, mix together the corn bread or corn bread stuffing mix, water, melted butter or margarine, bell pepper and reserved sausage. Pack loosely into the cavity of the chicken. Place the stuffed chicken in the pot. Bring to a simmer over medium-low heat, cover and simmer for 1 hour.

Using a large spoon, skim off any fat from the surface of the stock. Add the rosemary, carrots and potatoes and bring to a simmer. Re-cover and continue to simmer over medium-low heat until the chicken is cooked and the vegetables are tender, 45–60 minutes longer. To test the chicken, make a cut near the thigh joint; the meat should be opaque throughout. Season to taste with salt and pepper.

To serve, carve the chicken meat and place some meat, stuffing and vegetables on warmed plates.

Serves 4

23

Old-fashioned Chicken Stew with Dumplings

4–5 lb (2–2.5 kg) chicken breast halves, with skin intact

1 celery stalk with leaves, plus additional leaves for garnish, optional

1 yellow onion, sliced

1 teaspoon salt

4 white boiling potatoes, peeled and cut into bite-sized pieces

4 carrots, peeled and cut into slices ½ inch (12 mm) thick

3 tablespoons butter or margarine

⅓ cup (2 oz/60 g) all-purpose (plain) flour

1½ cups (12 fl oz/375 ml) light (single) cream

¼ teaspoon white pepper

1 lb (500 g) pearl onions, peeled (*see glossary, page 106*)

old-fashioned dumplings, steamed on a plate (*recipe on page 13*)

*I*n an 8-qt (8-l) heavy-bottomed stew pot, combine the chicken, celery, sliced onion, salt and water to cover. Bring to a boil, reduce the heat to medium-low, cover and simmer until the chicken is barely cooked, 20–25 minutes. Using tongs, transfer the chicken to a plate; set aside.

Remove the liquid from the heat and strain through a fine-mesh sieve into a clean container. Cool the liquid briefly, then cover and refrigerate until a layer of fat solidifies on top. Meanwhile, skin the chicken breasts and remove the meat from the bones in large pieces, then cover and refrigerate.

Using a slotted spoon, lift off the fat from the surface of the cooled stock and reserve. Bring the stock to a boil. Add the potatoes and carrots and boil for 15 minutes. Drain off the stock into a clean container; set the stock and vegetables aside separately.

In a 2-qt (2-l) saucepan over medium heat, melt the butter or margarine with 3 tablespoons of the reserved chicken fat. Whisk in the flour and cook, whisking constantly, for 2–3 minutes; do not brown. Slowly add 2½ cups (20 fl oz/625 ml) of the reserved stock and the cream, whisking constantly until smooth and slightly thickened, about 2 minutes. (Reserve any remaining stock for another use.) Stir in the white pepper, then pour the sauce over the potatoes and carrots. Add the reserved chicken and the pearl onions and bring to a gentle simmer. Cover and simmer over medium-low heat until the chicken is cooked through and the vegetables are tender when pierced with a fork, 20–30 minutes.

Begin steaming the dumplings on a plate about 20 minutes before the stew is ready. To serve, spoon the stew into bowls and slide the dumplings on top. Garnish with celery leaves, if desired.

Serves 8

Chicken with Mango, Sweet Potato and Cashews

3 tablespoons vegetable oil

4 skinless, boneless chicken breast halves, about 1½ lb (750 g) total weight, cut into 1-inch (2.5-cm) pieces

1 cup (8 fl oz/250 ml) orange juice

2 teaspoons cornstarch (cornflour)

1 clove garlic, finely chopped

1 large sweet onion, cut into 1-inch (2.5-cm) pieces

4 sweet potatoes, peeled and cut into 1-inch (2.5-cm) pieces

1 large ripe mango, peeled and cut off the pit into slices about ½ inch (12 mm) thick

1 cup (8 fl oz/250 ml) chicken stock (recipe on page 9)

½ teaspoon curry powder

½ cup (2½ oz/75 g) cashew nuts

2 green (spring) onions, including tender green tops, finely chopped

salt and freshly ground pepper

This dish is a lovely combination of the tastes of the Caribbean. If you like, garnish the stew with toasted coconut or banana chips, which are available in most food stores.

In a 4-qt (4-l) heavy-bottomed stew pot over medium-high heat, warm 2 tablespoons of the vegetable oil. Add the chicken pieces and sauté, stirring, until lightly golden, about 5 minutes. Using a slotted spoon, transfer to a dish. Add all but 2 table–spoons of the orange juice to the pot and, using a large spoon, deglaze the pot over medium-high heat by stirring to dislodge any browned bits from the pot bottom. In a small bowl, stir together the cornstarch and the reserved 2 tablespoons orange juice until the cornstarch is dissolved. Add the mixture to the pot and stir over medium-high heat until slightly thickened, 2–3 minutes. Pour the liquid over the chicken. Wipe the pot clean.

In the same pot over medium heat, warm the remaining 1 tablespoon oil. Add the garlic, onion and sweet potatoes and sauté until the onion is translucent, about 5 minutes. Return the chicken and juices to the pot and add the mango slices, chicken stock and curry powder. Stir well and bring to a simmer. Cover and simmer over medium-low heat until the sweet potatoes are tender and the chicken is cooked through, about 30 minutes.

Meanwhile, preheat an oven to 350°F (180°C). Spread the cashews on a baking sheet and bake until lightly toasted, about 5 minutes. Remove from the oven and set aside.

Remove the pot from the heat and stir in the green onions and toasted cashews. Season to taste with salt and pepper. Spoon into warmed shallow bowls and serve.

Serves 4

Cornish Hens with Green Peppercorns

2 Cornish hens, about 1⅔ lb (815 g) each

2 tablespoons olive oil

1 large sweet onion, cut into wedges 1 inch (2.5 cm) thick

2 cups (16 fl oz/500 ml) chicken stock (recipe on page 9)

1 cup (7 oz/220 g) medium-grain brown rice

2 or 3 oil-packed sun-dried tomatoes, drained and coarsely chopped

1 tablespoon drained brine-packed green peppercorns, rinsed and crushed with the flat side of a heavy knife blade

4 carrots, peeled and cut into 1-inch (2.5-cm) pieces

salt and freshly ground pepper

If you substitute purchased chicken stock in place of homemade, reduce the sun-dried tomatoes to 1 tablespoon chopped, to compensate for the saltiness of the commercial stock. For a colorful and impressive presentation, serve the hens over a bed of steamed, julienned zucchini (courgettes) and yellow squash and spoon the rice mixture around the edges.

*P*at the Cornish hens dry with paper towels. In a 4-qt (4-l) heavy-bottomed stew pot over medium-high heat, warm the olive oil. Add the hens and brown on all sides until golden, about 8 minutes. Using tongs, transfer the hens to a dish. Pour off the fat from the pot.

In the same pot over medium heat, add the onion and 2–3 tablespoons of the chicken stock and, using a large spoon, deglaze the pot by stirring to dislodge any browned bits from the pot bottom. Add the brown rice, sun-dried tomatoes, green peppercorns, carrots and the remaining stock. Bring to a boil over high heat. Reduce the heat to medium-low and return the hens to the pot. Cover and simmer gently until the hens are cooked and the rice is tender, 50–60 minutes. To test the hens, make a cut near the thigh joint with a sharp knife; the meat should be opaque throughout. Season to taste with salt and pepper.

To serve four, cut each hen in half before serving. Place each hen, or hen half, in a warmed shallow bowl and spoon the rice mixture around it.

Makes 2 very generous servings or 4 average servings

Duck in Red Wine with Apricots and Prunes

2 tablespoons butter or margarine

1 duck, 4–5 lb (2–2.5 kg), quartered, skinned and trimmed of fat

6 shallots, finely chopped

2 cloves garlic, minced

½ cup (3 oz/90 g) pitted prunes

½ cup (3 oz/90 g) dried apricots

¾ cup (6 fl oz/180 ml) dry red wine

1 cup (8 fl oz/250 ml) chicken stock *(recipe on page 9)*

salt and freshly ground pepper

The hearty pairing of duck and dried fruits makes this thick stew a perfect winter party dish. Try adding dried apples and dried cranberries as well. Serve it over a mixture of wild and white rice or mashed sweet potatoes.

In a 4-qt (4-l) heavy-bottomed stew pot over medium-high heat, melt the butter or margarine. Add the duck pieces, shallots and garlic and sauté, stirring, until lightly golden, about 10 minutes.

Pour off the duck fat from the pot and place the pot over medium-high heat. Add the prunes, apricots, red wine and chicken stock and, using a large spoon, deglaze the pot by stirring to dislodge any browned bits from the pot bottom. Reduce the heat to medium-low, cover and simmer gently for 30 minutes.

Turn the duck pieces over, re-cover and continue to simmer gently until the duck is tender and cooked through when pierced with a sharp knife, 30 minutes longer. Season to taste with salt and pepper.

Spoon into warmed shallow bowls and serve.

Serves 3 or 4

Portuguese Stew with Turkey Sausage

1 cup (7 oz/220 g) small dried white
  beans such as soldier or navy, or
  1 can (20 oz/625 g) chick-peas
  (garbanzo beans)
2 tablespoons olive oil
1 lb (500 g) spicy turkey sausages
1 large sweet onion, cut in half and
  then into slices ¼ inch (6 mm) thick
2 cups (16 fl oz/500 ml) chicken stock
  (recipe on page 9)
1 green bell pepper (capsicum), seeded,
  deribbed and cut lengthwise into
  strips ½ inch (12 mm) wide
2 cups (10 oz/315 g) cubed, peeled
  butternut (pumpkin) squash or
  sweet potato
1 can (28 oz/875 g) whole tomatoes in
  purée, with juices
½ teaspoon dried thyme
¼ teaspoon ground cayenne pepper
bouquet garni (recipe on page 10)
1 bunch kale leaves, separated and thick
  stems removed (about 1¼ lb/625 g)
salt and freshly ground pepper

Serve this heart-friendly update of a classic recipe with hot, crusty Italian bread. Look for turkey sausage in most markets. If unavailable, substitute spicy Italian pork sausage.

*I*f using white beans, pick over and discard any damaged beans or stones. Rinse the beans. Place in a bowl, add plenty of water to cover and let stand for about 3 hours. Drain the beans and place in a saucepan with water to cover by 2 inches (5 cm). Bring to a boil, reduce the heat to low and simmer gently, uncovered, until tender, 1–1½ hours. Drain the beans and set aside. Alternatively, drain the canned chick-peas and set aside.

In an 8-qt (8-l) heavy-bottomed stew pot over medium-high heat, warm the olive oil. Add the sausages and brown on all sides until golden, about 5 minutes. Using tongs, transfer to a dish and cut crosswise into pieces ½ inch (12 mm) thick; set aside.

In the same pot over medium-high heat, add the onion slices and sauté, stirring, until soft and the browned bits from the pot bottom begin to cling to the slices, about 8 minutes. Add 2–3 tablespoons of the chicken stock if needed to keep the onion from sticking. Slowly add the remaining stock, scraping the pot bottom with a large spoon.

Return the sausage to the pot, along with the bell pepper, squash or sweet potato, tomatoes and juices, thyme, cayenne pepper, bouquet garni, kale and the reserved beans. Stir well and bring to a simmer. Cover and simmer gently over medium-low heat until the kale is tender and the flavors have developed, about 45 minutes. Season to taste with salt and pepper.

Spoon into warmed bowls and serve.

Serves 4–6

Chicken Curry

2 tablespoons olive oil

4 skinless, boneless chicken breast halves, about 1½ lb (750 g) total weight, cut into bite-sized pieces

2 cloves garlic, finely chopped

1 tart red apple such as Cortland or Empire, quartered, cored and coarsely chopped

1 large sweet onion, coarsely chopped

1 large green bell pepper (capsicum), seeded, deribbed and coarsely chopped

4 plum (Roma) tomatoes, quartered lengthwise

2 teaspoons curry powder

½ teaspoon peeled and finely chopped fresh ginger

salt and freshly ground pepper

To give this thick and fragrant stew an authentic touch, serve it with steamed white rice and an assortment of traditional condiments: toasted coconut, mango chutney, raisins and sliced bananas or apples. Garnish with apple slices, if desired.

In a 4-qt (4-l) heavy-bottomed stew pot over medium heat, warm the olive oil. Add the chicken pieces and sauté, stirring, until lightly browned, 8–10 minutes. Using a slotted spoon, transfer the chicken to a bowl.

Add the garlic, apple and onion to the same pot over medium heat and sauté, stirring, until the onion is translucent, about 5 minutes. Return the chicken to the pot. Add the bell pepper, tomatoes, curry powder and ginger. Bring to a simmer. Reduce the heat to medium-low, cover and simmer gently for 10 minutes, to blend and develop the flavors. Season to taste with salt and pepper.

Spoon into warmed shallow bowls and serve.

Serves 4

Chicken with Okra

2 tablespoons olive oil
4 skinless, boneless chicken breast
  halves, about 1½ lb (750 g) total
  weight, cut into 1-inch (2.5-cm)
  pieces
1 large sweet onion, cut into wedges
  1 inch (2.5 cm) thick
½ lb (250 g) okra, trimmed and cut
  crosswise into slices ¼ inch (6 mm)
  thick
1 can (28 oz/875 g) whole tomatoes in
  purée, with juices
½ teaspoon ground coriander
salt and freshly ground pepper

Okra adds flavor and a unique texture to this dish adapted from West African kitchens. Serve it spooned over toasted thick slices of French bread or steamed rice and garnish with flat-leaf (Italian) parsley.

In a 4-qt (4-l) heavy-bottomed stew pot over medium-high heat, warm the olive oil. Add the chicken pieces and sauté, stirring, until golden brown, about 8 minutes. Using a slotted spoon, transfer the chicken to a dish.

Reduce the heat to medium and add the onion to the same pot. Sauté, stirring, until translucent, about 5 minutes. Add the okra and sauté, stirring, for about 5 minutes longer, scraping the bottom of the pan as necessary to keep the okra from sticking.

Add the tomatoes, breaking the large ones in half, and their juices. Return the chicken to the pot, then add the coriander. Stir well and bring to a simmer. Reduce the heat to medium-low, cover and simmer gently until the okra has softened and the juices have thickened slightly, about 20 minutes. Season to taste with salt and pepper.

Spoon into warmed shallow bowls and serve.

Serves 4

Chicken Marsala

1 cup (5 oz/155 g) all-purpose (plain) flour

1 teaspoon salt

1 teaspoon dried basil

4 skinless, boneless chicken breast halves, about 1½ lb (750 g) total weight

¼ cup (2 fl oz/60 ml) olive oil

2 cloves garlic, chopped

2 tablespoons butter or margarine

10 oz (315 g) small fresh white mushroom caps (about 3 cups)

½ cup (4 fl oz/125 ml) sweet Marsala wine or sweet sherry

This oven-baked stew combines tender pieces of herb-crusted chicken breasts and a rich wine-mushroom sauce. If you like, serve it over an herbed rice pilaf or steamed white rice studded with toasted blanched almonds.

Preheat an oven to 350°F (180°C). Spray a 9-by-13-inch (23-by-33-cm) rectangular or oval baking dish with vegetable oil cooking spray (or grease with vegetable oil).

In a sturdy brown paper bag, combine the flour, salt and basil. Fold the top over tightly and shake to mix. Cut the chicken breasts crosswise into thirds. Working in batches of three or four at a time, add the chicken pieces to the bag and shake until well coated.

In a large, heavy frying pan over medium-high heat, warm the olive oil. Add the garlic and the chicken pieces and sauté, stirring, until the chicken is golden brown, about 8 minutes. Scrape the bottom of the pan frequently to dislodge any browned bits. Remove from the heat and transfer the chicken and garlic to the prepared baking dish.

Return the pan to medium-high heat and add the butter or margarine. When it melts, add the mushrooms and sauté, stirring gently, for 2–3 minutes. Pour in the Marsala or sherry and, using a large spoon, deglaze the pan by stirring to dislodge any browned bits from the pan bottom. Pour the liquid and mushrooms over the chicken.

Cover the baking dish with aluminum foil and bake until the chicken is cooked, about 20 minutes. To test, cut into a piece of chicken with sharp knife; the meat should be opaque throughout.

Spoon into warmed bowls and serve.

Serves 4

Paprika Veal Stew with Dumplings

2 tablespoons olive oil

1½ lb (750 g) boneless veal shoulder, cut into 1-inch (2.5-cm) cubes

1 large sweet onion, cut in half lengthwise and then crosswise into slices ¼ inch (6 mm) thick

1 tablespoon Hungarian paprika

½ teaspoon dried thyme

1 can (28 oz/875 g) whole tomatoes in purée, with juices

old-fashioned dumplings, steamed on a plate *(recipe on page 13)*

1 cup (8 fl oz/250 ml) sour cream

salt and freshly ground pepper

fresh thyme sprigs, optional

Hungarian paprika gives this well-known dish an especially vibrant color and superior flavor, although any type of paprika may be substituted. Be sure your paprika has not sat on the shelf too long or its potency will have diminished. If you must reheat the stew, use low heat and do not allow it to boil or the sour cream will curdle.

◆

*I*n a 4-qt (4-l) heavy-bottomed stew pot over medium-high heat, warm the olive oil. Working in batches if necessary, add the veal cubes and brown on all sides, about 5 minutes. Add the onion slices and sauté, stirring, until soft and the browned bits from the pot bottom begin to cling to them, about 5 minutes. Stir in the paprika, thyme and tomatoes and juices, breaking up the tomatoes in the pan with the spoon. Bring to a simmer, reduce the heat to medium-low, cover and simmer gently until the veal is tender, 40–60 minutes.

About 20 minutes before the veal is done, steam the dumplings on a plate. When the veal is done, remove the pot from the heat and stir in the sour cream. Season to taste with salt and pepper.

Spoon the stew into warmed shallow bowls and slide the dumplings on top. Garnish with thyme sprigs, if desired, and serve immediately.

Serves 4

Pork with Prunes and Apple Brandy

1 tablespoon olive oil

1½ lb (750 g) lean pork tenderloin, trimmed of fat and cut into 1½-inch (4-cm) cubes

½ cup (4 fl oz/125 ml) apple brandy or Calvados

1 tablespoon butter or margarine

1 large sweet onion, cut in half lengthwise and then crosswise into slices ¼ inch (6 mm) thick

4 carrots, peeled and cut into 1-inch (2.5-cm) pieces

1 cup (8 fl oz/250 ml) apple juice

2 cups (12 oz/375 g) pitted prunes

salt and freshly ground pepper

Dried fruit, fresh vegetables and pork tenderloin are spiked with apple brandy in this delicious stew. Calvados, from the region of Normandy in northwestern France, is the best-quality apple brandy you can use, although any variety will work. Baked sweet potatoes and applesauce make excellent accompaniments.

◆

*I*n a 4-qt (4-l) heavy-bottomed stew pot over medium-high heat, warm the olive oil. Working in batches if necessary, add the pork cubes and brown lightly on all sides, 3–4 minutes. Using a slotted spoon, transfer the pork to a dish and set aside. Pour off the oil from the pot and place the pot over medium-high heat. Add the apple brandy and, using a large spoon, deglaze the pot by stirring to dislodge any browned bits from the pot bottom. Pour the liquid over the pork, then wipe the pot clean.

In the same pot over medium heat, melt the butter or margarine. Add the onion and sauté, stirring, until translucent, about 5 minutes. Return the pork and juices to the pot. Add the carrots, apple juice and prunes and bring to a simmer. Reduce the heat to medium-low, cover and simmer gently until the pork and vegetables are tender, about 40 minutes. Season to taste with salt and pepper.

Spoon into warmed shallow bowls or plates and serve.

Serves 4–6

Pork and Papaya

¼ cup (1½ oz/45 g) all-purpose (plain) flour

1 lb (500 g) lean pork tenderloin, cut into 1-inch (2.5-cm) cubes

2 tablespoons butter or margarine

2 shallots, finely chopped

2 papayas, peeled, halved lengthwise, seeded and cut crosswise into slices ½ inch (12 mm) thick

2 tablespoons fresh lime juice

bouquet garni *(recipe on page 10)*, substituting 6 whole cloves for the garlic

1½ cups (12 fl oz/375 ml) chicken stock *(recipe on page 9)*

½ cup (4 fl oz/125 ml) sweet white wine

½ lb (250 g) green beans, trimmed and cut into 2-inch (5-cm) lengths (optional)

3 or 4 dashes hot-pepper sauce, such as Tabasco

salt and freshly ground pepper

2 tablespoons finely chopped fresh chives

Peaches can be substituted for the papayas in this recipe; use 4 peaches, peeled, pitted and sliced, and omit the lime juice. Creamy mashed potatoes speckled with bits of chopped fresh chives make a delicious bed for this colorful stew.

*P*lace the flour on a plate and coat the pork cubes with the flour. In a 4-qt (4-l) heavy-bottomed stew pot over medium-high heat, melt the butter or margarine. Add the pork and brown on all sides, about 5 minutes.

Meanwhile, in a bowl, toss the shallots and papayas with the lime juice. When the pork is browned, add the shallots and papayas, the bouquet garni, chicken stock and wine. Bring to a simmer, reduce the heat to medium-low, cover and simmer gently until the pork is tender, 35–40 minutes. If desired, add the green beans during the last 15 minutes of cooking.

When the stew is ready, remove the bouquet garni and discard. Add the hot-pepper sauce and season to taste with salt and pepper.

To serve, spoon into warmed shallow bowls or plates and garnish with the chives.

Serves 4

Beef Stew in a Pumpkin

1 sugar pumpkin or butternut squash,
  about 5 lb (2.5 kg)

1 tablespoon vegetable oil

1 lb (500 g) beef top round, trimmed
  of fat and cut into ½-inch (12-mm)
  cubes

1¾ cups (14 fl oz/440 ml) beef stock
  (recipe on page 9)

1 tablespoon butter or margarine

3 yellow onions, cut in half and then
  into slices ½ inch (12 mm) thick

3 small parsnips, peeled and coarsely
  chopped

½ teaspoon ground cinnamon

¼ teaspoon freshly grated nutmeg

¼ cup (2 fl oz/60 ml) bourbon or
  other whiskey

2 tablespoons brown sugar

salt and freshly ground pepper

Sugar pumpkin, a mildly sweet pumpkin variety, provides a beautiful serving container for this chunky stew. Bourbon, an American whiskey, imparts a touch of sweet, smoky flavor.

◆

*P*reheat an oven to 350°F (180°C).

Cut a 4-inch (10-cm) diameter circle around the stem of the pumpkin or squash and lift it off. Discard the pumpkin top or set it aside to use as a lid. Scoop out and discard the seeds. Line the bottom and sides of a shallow baking pan with aluminum foil and spray it with a vegetable oil cooking spray (or grease with vegetable oil). Place the pumpkin or squash in the baking pan and set aside.

In a 4-qt (4-l) heavy-bottomed stew pot over medium-high heat, warm the vegetable oil. Add the beef cubes and brown well on all sides, about 5 minutes. Using a slotted spoon, transfer the beef to a dish. Pour the beef stock into the pot and, using a large spoon, deglaze the pot over medium-high heat by stirring to dislodge any browned bits from the pot bottom. Pour the liquid over the beef, then wipe the pot clean.

In the same pot over medium heat, melt the butter or margarine. Add the onions and parsnips and sauté, stirring, until the onions are browned lightly, about 15 minutes.

Return the beef and juices to the pot and add the cinnamon, nutmeg and bourbon. Mix well and then spoon the beef mixture into the pumpkin or squash. Sprinkle the brown sugar over the top. Bake until the pumpkin or squash is soft when pierced with a fork and the meat is tender, 2–2½ hours. About 45 minutes before the stew is done, place the pumpkin lid, if using, on the baking sheet and bake until tender, about 45 minutes. Season the stew to taste with salt and pepper and top with the pumpkin lid, if using.

Spoon into warmed bowls at the table and serve immediately.

Serves 4

Irish Lamb Stew

2 lb (1 kg) boneless lamb shoulder,
  trimmed of fat and cut into 1-inch
  (2.5-cm) cubes

4 white boiling potatoes, peeled and
  cut crosswise into slices ½ inch
  (12 mm) thick

2 yellow onions, cut in half lengthwise
  and then crosswise into slices ½ inch
  (12 mm) thick

1 large turnip, cut crosswise into slices
  ¼ inch (6 mm) thick

2 fresh thyme sprigs or ¼ teaspoon
  dried thyme

3 fresh parsley sprigs

1 teaspoon salt

¼ teaspoon freshly ground pepper

This layered stew cooks for several hours, rendering especially tender results. Offer thick slices of Irish soda bread or buttermilk biscuits alongside for sopping up all the juices, and garnish each serving with a sprig of parsley.

In a 4-qt (4-l) heavy-bottomed stew pot, rinse the meat by combining the lamb cubes with water to cover. Drain off the water and then again add water to cover by 1 inch (2.5 cm). Bring to a boil over high heat and boil for 5 minutes. Using a slotted spoon, transfer the lamb to a dish. Pour the broth into a separate bowl and set aside.

Layer half of the potato slices in the bottom of the same pot. Cover with half of the onion slices and then top with all of the turnip slices. Distribute the lamb evenly over the turnips and top with the thyme, parsley, salt and pepper. Top with the remaining onions and finally the remaining potatoes. Strain the broth through a fine-mesh sieve over the potatoes.

Bring to a low boil over high heat. Reduce the heat to medium-low, cover and simmer gently until the lamb is tender when pierced, about 2 hours.

Spoon into warmed bowls, discarding the thyme and parsley sprigs, and serve.

Serves 4–6

Beef Stew with Tomatoes

2 tablespoons olive oil

1½ lb (750 g) beef bottom round

1 large sweet onion, cut in half and then into slices ½ inch (12 mm) thick

1 can (28 oz/875 g) whole tomatoes in purée, with juices

1 tablespoon red wine vinegar

2 tablespoons brown sugar

½ teaspoon ground ginger

1 teaspoon ground cinnamon

1 bay leaf

4 large carrots, peeled and cut into 1-inch (2.5-cm) pieces

4 white boiling potatoes, peeled and cut into 1-inch (2.5-cm) cubes

salt and freshly ground pepper

The addition of cinnamon imparts a mild sweetness to this aromatic stew. Serve it over a bed of steamed white rice, if you like.

◈

*I*n an 8-qt (8-l) heavy-bottomed stew pot over medium-high heat, warm the olive oil. Add the beef and brown well on all sides, about 5 minutes. Add the onion and sauté, stirring, until softened, 2–3 minutes. Add the tomatoes and juices, vinegar, brown sugar, ginger, cinnamon and the bay leaf and stir well. Bring to a simmer, reduce the heat to medium-low, cover and simmer gently for 30 minutes.

Add the carrots and potatoes and continue to simmer gently until the meat and vegetables are tender, about 1 hour longer. Discard the bay leaf and season to taste with salt and pepper.

To serve, transfer the meat to a cutting board. Cut across the grain into thick slices. Place the slices in warmed bowls and spoon the vegetable mixture over the top.

Serves 4

Chinese Beef Stew with Five-Spice Powder

1 tablespoon vegetable oil

1½ lb (750 g) beef sirloin tip, cut into strips ½ inch (12 mm) thick and 3 inches (7.5 cm) long

2 cups (16 fl oz/500 ml) beef stock (recipe on page 9)

¼ cup (2 fl oz/60 ml) soy sauce

2 tablespoons dry sherry

1 piece fresh ginger, about 1 inch (2.5 cm) long, unpeeled and sliced lengthwise into julienne strips ¼ inch (6 mm) thick

½–¾ teaspoon Chinese five-spice powder

1½ lb (750 g) mild Chinese radish (lo bok), peeled, cut in half lengthwise and then cut crosswise into 2-inch (5-cm) pieces

4 green (spring) onions, including tender green tops, cut into 2-inch (5-cm) lengths

5 or 6 leaves Chinese (napa) cabbage, cut crosswise into strips 2 inches (5 cm) wide

The exotic ingredients called for in this recipe are easily found in a market that specializes in Asian foods. The Chinese radish, called lo bok *in Cantonese, is sweeter than its more popular cousin, the Japanese daikon. Any mild sweet turnip may be substituted for the Chinese radish.*

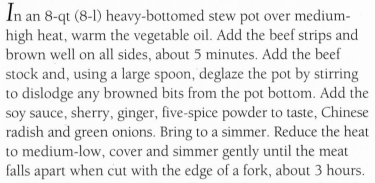

*I*n an 8-qt (8-l) heavy-bottomed stew pot over medium-high heat, warm the vegetable oil. Add the beef strips and brown well on all sides, about 5 minutes. Add the beef stock and, using a large spoon, deglaze the pot by stirring to dislodge any browned bits from the pot bottom. Add the soy sauce, sherry, ginger, five-spice powder to taste, Chinese radish and green onions. Bring to a simmer. Reduce the heat to medium-low, cover and simmer gently until the meat falls apart when cut with the edge of a fork, about 3 hours.

Using a large spoon, skim off the fat from the surface of the stew. Add the cabbage, cover and continue to simmer over medium-low heat until the cabbage is very soft and wilted but not mushy, about 30 minutes longer.

Spoon into warmed shallow bowls and serve.

Serves 4–6

Sweet-and-Sour Brisket

1 beef brisket, 5–6 lb (2.5–3 kg)

2 large sweet onions, cut in half lengthwise and then crosswise into slices about ½ inch (12 mm) thick

4 celery stalks, cut into slices ½ inch (12 mm) thick (about 3 cups/12 oz/ 375 g)

1 cup (8 fl oz/250 ml) bottled chili sauce

½ cup (3½ oz/105 g) firmly packed brown sugar

⅓ cup (3 oz/90 g) Dijon-style mustard

¼ cup (2 fl oz/60 ml) red wine vinegar

3 tablespoons light (unsulfured) molasses

¼ cup (2 fl oz/60 ml) soy sauce

½ teaspoon paprika

1 can (12 fl oz/375 ml) beer

4 white boiling potatoes, peeled and thickly sliced

4 carrots, peeled and cut into 1-inch (2.5-cm) pieces

1 small head white cabbage, cored and tough outer leaves removed, cut into slices 1 inch (2.5 cm) thick

1 tablespoon caraway seeds

For this meat-and-potatoes favorite, make sure you buy a first-cut brisket, which is less fatty than other cuts.

◆

*I*n a dry, 4-qt (4-l) heavy-bottomed stew pot over medium-high heat, place the brisket, fat side down. Brown, turning once, until deep brown on both sides, about 6 minutes. Pour off the fat from the pot.

Add the onions, celery, chili sauce, brown sugar, mustard, vinegar, molasses, soy sauce, paprika and beer to the pot. Stir well and bring to a simmer. Reduce the heat to medium-low, cover and simmer gently for 3 hours.

Using a large spoon, skim off as much fat as possible from the top of the stew. Add the potatoes, carrots and cabbage and return to a simmer. Simmer gently, uncovered, over medium-low heat until the brisket falls apart easily when flaked with a fork and the vegetables are tender, about 1 hour.

To serve, transfer the brisket to a cutting board and cut across the grain into slices ½ inch (12 mm) thick. Stir the caraway seeds into the cabbage-vegetable mixture. Spoon the cabbage onto a warmed platter. Place the meat slices on the cabbage and arrange the vegetables alongside. Spoon any remaining pan juices over the top.

Serves 8

Greek Meatball Stew with Brussels Sprouts

1 lb (500 g) pearl onions
½ cup (2½ oz/75 g) finely chopped
   yellow onion
1 lb (500 g) ground (minced) lamb
   shoulder
⅔ cup (3½ oz/105 g) cooled, cooked
   white rice
3 tablespoons finely chopped fresh mint
¼ teaspoon freshly ground pepper
2 teaspoons olive oil
¼ cup (2 oz/60 g) butter or margarine
¼ cup (1½ oz/45 g) all-purpose (plain)
   flour
1½ cups (12 fl oz/375 ml) chicken
   stock (recipe on page 9)
¼ cup (2 fl oz/60 ml) fresh lemon juice
¾ lb (375 g) small fresh Brussels
   sprouts, trimmed, or 1 package
   (10 oz/315 g) frozen Brussels sprouts
salt and freshly ground pepper

Prepare this homey dish for an informal buffet dinner. Serve with wedges of pita bread, steamed white rice and a Greek salad, if you like.

Using a sharp knife, trim off the root ends of the pearl onions. Cut a shallow X in each trimmed end (to keep the onions whole during cooking). In a pot, combine the onions with plenty of water to cover. Bring to a boil and boil for about 2 minutes. Drain and, when cool enough to handle, slip off the skins. Set the onions aside.

In a bowl, combine the yellow onion, lamb, rice, mint and pepper. Mix well. Form spoonfuls of the mixture into thumb-shaped meatballs. In a 4-qt (4-l) heavy-bottomed stew pot over medium-high heat, warm the olive oil. Add the meatballs and brown on all sides, 3–4 minutes. Using a slotted spoon, transfer the meatballs to a dish, then wipe the pot clean.

In the same pot over medium heat, melt the butter or margarine. Whisk in the flour and cook, whisking constantly, for 2 minutes; do not allow to brown. Slowly pour in the chicken stock and lemon juice, whisking constantly until smooth and slightly thickened, 2–3 minutes.

Return the meatballs to the pot. Add the Brussels sprouts and the reserved pearl onions. Reduce the heat to medium-low, cover and simmer gently until the vegetables are tender and the meatballs are cooked through, 15–20 minutes. Season to taste with salt and pepper.

Spoon into warmed bowls and serve.

Serves 4–6

Beef Strips with Shallots

1 lb (500 g) pearl onions

1 tablespoon olive oil

2 lb (1 kg) beef top round, trimmed of
fat and cut into strips ½ inch (12 mm)
wide, ½–¾ inch (12 mm–2 cm) thick
and 3 inches (7.5 cm) long

½ cup (4 fl oz/125 ml) Burgundy or
other full-bodied dry red wine

2 tablespoons butter or margarine

½ cup (2 oz/60 g) shallots, left whole
or cut into halves or quarters if large

1 lb (500 g) baby carrots, peeled if
desired

10 oz (315 g) small fresh white
mushroom caps

1 cup (8 fl oz/250 ml) beef stock
(recipe on page 9)

½ teaspoon dried thyme

1 tablespoon cornstarch (cornflour)
dissolved in 1 tablespoon cold water

salt and freshly ground pepper

To save time, purchase precut beef strips, which are available in many markets, or have your butcher prepare them for you. Serve the stew over rice or orzo as the centerpiece of an elegant dinner party.

Using a sharp knife, trim off the root ends of the pearl onions. Cut a shallow X in each trimmed end (to keep the onions whole during cooking). In a pot, combine the onions with plenty of water to cover. Bring to a boil. Boil for about 2 minutes. Drain and, when cool enough to handle, slip off the skins. Set the onions aside.

In an 8-qt (8-l) heavy-bottomed stew pot over medium-high heat, warm the olive oil. Add the beef strips and brown well on all sides, about 5 minutes. Using a slotted spoon, transfer the beef to a dish and set aside. Pour the wine into the pot and, using a large spoon, deglaze the pot over medium-high heat by stirring to dislodge any browned bits from the pot bottom. Pour the liquid over the beef strips, then wipe the pot clean.

In the same pot over medium heat, melt the butter or margarine. Add the shallots and reserved pearl onions and sauté until the shallots are translucent, about 5 minutes. Add the carrots and mushrooms and sauté, stirring, until the mushrooms are lightly golden, about 5 minutes longer.

Return the beef and juices to the pot and add the beef stock and thyme. Bring to a simmer. Reduce the heat to medium-low, cover and simmer gently until the beef is tender when pierced with a fork, about 25 minutes.

Stir in the cornstarch mixture and cook over medium heat, stirring occasionally, until thickened, about 5 minutes. Season to taste with salt and pepper.

Spoon into warmed bowls and serve.

Serves 6

Italian Beef Stew

3 tablespoons olive oil

1 beef chuck steak, 2 lb (1 kg), trimmed of fat

2 tablespoons red wine vinegar

2 large sweet onions, cut in half lengthwise and then crosswise into slices ½ inch (12 mm) thick

2 long Italian red sweet peppers (capsicums) or red bell peppers, seeded, deribbed and cut crosswise into strips ½ inch (12 mm) wide

2 green bell peppers (capsicums), seeded, deribbed and cut lengthwise into strips 1 inch (2.5 cm) wide

2 cups (16 fl oz/500 ml) beef stock (recipe on page 9)

½ lb (250 g) Italian (romano) green beans, ends trimmed, cut into 2-inch (5-cm) lengths

1 can (8 oz/250 g) straw mushrooms, drained

salt and freshly ground pepper

Long cooking at a low temperature makes chuck steak wonderfully tender. If you cannot find the Italian green beans, substitute regular green beans, but reduce the cooking time to about 15 minutes.

◆

*I*n a 4-qt (4-l) heavy-bottomed stew pot over medium-high heat, warm 1 tablespoon of the olive oil. Place the chuck steak in the pot and brown, turning once, until richly browned on both sides, 4–6 minutes. Transfer the chuck steak to a dish. Add the vinegar to the pot and, using a large spoon, deglaze the pot over medium-high heat by stirring to dislodge any browned bits from the pot bottom. Pour the liquid over the steak.

In the same pot over medium-high heat, warm the remaining 2 tablespoons oil. Add the onions and the red and green peppers and sauté, stirring, until well browned, about 10 minutes. Add 2–3 tablespoons water if necessary to keep the vegetables from sticking.

Slowly stir in the beef stock, scraping the pot bottom at the same time to dislodge any browned bits. Return the meat to the pot and bring to a simmer. Reduce the heat to medium-low, cover and simmer gently until the meat is very tender when pierced with a fork, about 2½ hours.

Add the green beans, re-cover and simmer gently until the beans are just tender, 20–30 minutes longer. Transfer the meat to a cutting board and cut it into bite-sized pieces. Return the meat to the pot over medium heat. Add the mushrooms and continue to simmer, stirring gently, until the mushrooms and meat are heated through, 2–3 minutes. Season to taste with salt and pepper.

Spoon into warmed bowls and serve.

Serves 4

Beef and Rosemary with Red Potatoes

2 tablespoons olive oil

2 cloves garlic, minced

1½ lb (750 g) beef bottom round, cut
into 1-inch (2.5-cm) cubes

½ cup (4 fl oz/125 ml) dry red wine

1 cup (8 fl oz/250 ml) beef stock
(recipe on page 9)

10 small red potatoes, unpeeled

2 tablespoons fresh rosemary leaves or
2 teaspoons dried rosemary

salt and freshly ground pepper

Rosemary is the special touch that gives this traditional beef stew its distinctive taste. Beef bottom round is a cut well suited to stews, as it becomes tender through long cooking and readily accepts other flavors.

◈

*I*n a 4-qt (4-l) heavy-bottomed stew pot over medium-high heat, warm the olive oil. Add the garlic and beef cubes and cook, stirring, until the beef is lightly browned and the garlic is golden but not dark brown, 3–4 minutes.

Pour in the wine and, using a large spoon, deglaze the pot over medium-high heat by stirring to dislodge any browned bits from the pan bottom. Add the beef stock and stir well.

Add the potatoes and sprinkle with the rosemary. Bring to a simmer. Reduce the heat to medium-low, cover and simmer gently until the beef and potatoes are tender when pierced with a fork, 25–30 minutes. Season to taste with salt and pepper.

Spoon into warmed bowls and serve.

Serves 4

Pork and Parsnips in Sherry

2 tablespoons olive oil

2 lb (1 kg) lean pork tenderloin, cut into 1-inch (2.5-cm) cubes

⅔ cup (5 fl oz/160 ml) dry sherry

1 tablespoon butter or margarine

4 shallots, chopped

6 small parsnips, peeled and quartered

4 sweet potatoes or small yams, peeled and cut into bite-sized pieces

2½ cups (20 fl oz/625 ml) vegetable or chicken stock *(recipes on pages 8–9)*

2 tablespoons maple syrup

2 tablespoons finely chopped fresh parsley or 1 teaspoon dried parsley

salt and freshly ground pepper

The combination of maple syrup and dry sherry provides a mildly sweet and wonderfully mellow accent. Serve over steamed rice or cooked egg noodles and garnish with a sprinkling of chopped fresh parsley.

◆

*I*n a 4-qt (4-l) heavy-bottomed stew pot over medium-high heat, warm the olive oil. Working in batches if necessary, add the pork cubes and brown lightly on all sides, 3–4 minutes. Using a slotted spoon, transfer the pork to a dish. Pour the sherry into the pot and, using a large spoon, deglaze the pot over medium-high heat by stirring to dislodge any browned bits from the pot bottom. Pour the liquid over the pork, then wipe the pot clean.

In the same pot over medium heat, melt the butter or margarine. Add the shallots, parsnips and sweet potatoes or yams and sauté, stirring, until the shallots are golden brown, about 10 minutes. Return the pork and juices to the pot and add the vegetable or chicken stock, maple syrup and parsley. Stir well and bring to a simmer. Reduce the heat to medium-low, cover and simmer gently until the pork is tender when pierced with a fork, 40–45 minutes. Season to taste with salt and pepper.

Spoon into warmed shallow bowls and serve.

Serves 6

Pork and Endive with Juniper Berries

2 tablespoons butter or margarine

1 lb (500 g) lean pork tenderloin, trimmed of fat and cut into 1-inch (2.5-cm) cubes

2 large sweet onions, cut in half and then into slices ½ inch (12 mm) thick

2 cups (16 fl oz/500 ml) chicken stock *(recipe on page 9)*

1 tablespoon juniper berries

4 heads Belgian endive (chicory/witloof)

2 tablespoons light brown sugar

1 teaspoon soy sauce

salt and freshly ground pepper

The combination of slightly sweet and bitter accents in this simple-to-assemble dish is divine. Pork tenderloin makes an especially tender stew meat that readily accepts the essence of the ingredients with which it is cooked. Juniper berries can be found in well-stocked markets or in specialty-food stores.

◈

In a 4-qt (4-l) heavy-bottomed stew pot over medium heat, melt the butter or margarine. Add the pork cubes and brown on all sides, 3–5 minutes. Add the onions and sauté, stirring, until they are slightly soft and the browned bits from the pot bottom begin to cling to them, 6–8 minutes.

Pour in the chicken stock and add the juniper berries, mixing well. Add the endives, pushing them down into the liquid so they are fully immersed. Bring to a simmer, reduce the heat to medium-low, cover and simmer gently until the pork is cooked through and the endives are tender, 30–40 minutes.

Add the brown sugar and soy sauce and stir until well mixed. Season to taste with salt and pepper.

Spoon into warmed bowls and serve.

Serves 4

Lamb Stew with Caramelized Onions

2 tablespoons olive oil

2 lb (1 kg) boneless lamb shoulder, trimmed of fat and cut into 1-inch (2.5-cm) cubes

4 sweet onions, cut in half lengthwise and then crosswise into slices ¼ inch (6 mm) thick

2 leeks, white part only, carefully washed and finely chopped

2 cups (16 fl oz/500 ml) vegetable stock *(recipe on page 8)* or water

6 white boiling potatoes, peeled and cut into 1-inch (2.5-cm) pieces

4 carrots, peeled and cut into 1-inch (2.5-cm) pieces

½ teaspoon dried thyme

1 bay leaf

salt and freshly ground pepper

Richly browned meat and caramelized onions lend deep color and wonderful richness to this substantial dish. Be careful not to brown the meat too much, however, or it will impart a burned taste to the other ingredients.

◈

In an 8-qt (8-l) heavy-bottomed stew pot over medium-high heat, warm the olive oil. Working in batches if necessary, add the lamb cubes and brown well on all sides, about 5 minutes. Using a slotted spoon, transfer the lamb to a dish.

Add the onions and leeks to the pot and sauté, stirring, until well browned, 10–12 minutes. Stir in 2–3 tablespoons of the stock or water if necessary to keep the vegetables from sticking or becoming too dark. They should be dark brown but not black; watch them carefully.

Add the remaining stock or water and bring to a simmer. Reduce the heat to medium-low, cover and simmer gently for 1 hour.

Add the reserved lamb, potatoes, carrots, thyme and bay leaf. Cover and continue to simmer gently until the meat is tender when pierced with a sharp fork, about 1 hour longer. Discard the bay leaf and season to taste with salt and pepper.

Spoon into warmed bowls and serve.

Serves 4

Veal Stew with Pearl Onions and Mushrooms

1 lb (500 g) pearl onions
¼ cup (1½ oz/45 g) all-purpose (plain)
  flour
1½ lb (750 g) boneless veal shoulder,
  cut into 1-inch (2.5-cm) cubes
3 tablespoons olive oil
1 cup (8 fl oz/250 ml) dry white wine
2 tablespoons butter or margarine
1 cup (8 fl oz/250 ml) vegetable stock
  (recipe on page 8)
3 cups (10 oz/315 g) small fresh white
  mushroom caps
½ teaspoon dried tarragon
¼ teaspoon white pepper
salt

A bed of steamed white rice or cooked egg noodles is a traditional accompaniment for this centuries-old favorite. Garnish it with a generous dollop of sour cream, a sprinkling of chopped fresh parsley and a few thin slices of lemon.

❖

Using a sharp knife, trim off the root ends of the onions. Cut a shallow X in each trimmed end (to keep the onions whole during cooking). In a pot, combine the onions with plenty of water to cover. Bring to a boil. Boil for about 2 minutes. Drain the onions and, when cool enough to handle, slip off the skins. Set the onions aside.

Place the flour on a plate; coat the veal cubes with the flour.

In a 4-qt (4-l) heavy-bottomed stew pot over medium-high heat, warm the olive oil. Add the veal cubes and brown lightly on all sides, about 4 minutes. Using a slotted spoon, transfer the veal to a dish and set aside.

Pour off the oil from the pot and place the pot over medium-high heat. Add 2–3 tablespoons of the wine and, using a large spoon, deglaze the pot by stirring to dislodge any browned bits from the pot bottom. Pour the liquid over the veal.

In the same pot over medium heat, melt the butter or margarine. Add the reserved pearl onions and sauté, stirring, until golden but not browned, about 5 minutes. Slowly add the stock and the remaining wine. Return the veal and juices to the pot and add the mushrooms, tarragon and white pepper. Stir well and bring to a simmer. Reduce the heat to medium-low, cover and simmer gently until the meat is tender when pierced with a fork, about 1 hour. Season to taste with salt.

Spoon into warmed shallow bowls or plates and serve.

Serves 4

Mediterranean Fish Stew

½ cup (2½ oz/75 g) all-purpose (plain) flour

1½ lb (750 g) tuna or swordfish steaks, each ¾–1 inch (2–2.5 cm) thick, cut into 1-inch (2.5-cm) chunks

2 tablespoons butter or margarine

3 tablespoons olive oil

1 cup (8 fl oz/250 ml) fish stock *(recipe on page 8)*

2 large sweet onions, cut in half lengthwise and then crosswise into slices ½ inch (12 mm) thick

1 green bell pepper (capsicum), seeded, deribbed and cut lengthwise into strips ½ inch (12 mm) wide

2 large tomatoes, cut into wedges ¾ inch (2 cm) thick

bouquet garni *(recipe on page 10)*

½ teaspoon dried basil

¼ teaspoon freshly ground pepper

¼ cup (1½ oz/45 g) pitted small green olives

¼ cup (1½ oz/45 g) pitted small black olives

In Italy, seafood stews like this one are traditionally ladled into shallow bowls atop thick slices of toasted bread that have been rubbed with fresh garlic and drizzled with oil. You may substitute any firm-textured fish steak for the tuna or swordfish.

※

Spread the flour on a plate and coat the fish pieces with the flour; shake off the excess flour.

In a 4-qt (4-l) heavy-bottomed stew pot over medium-high heat, melt the butter or margarine with 2 tablespoons of the olive oil. Add the fish and sauté, stirring, until lightly browned on all sides, about 5 minutes.

Transfer the fish and any pan juices to a dish. Add 2–3 tablespoons of the fish stock to the pot and, using a large spoon, deglaze the pot over medium-high heat by stirring to dislodge any browned bits from the pot bottom. Pour the liquid over the fish.

Reduce the heat to medium and add the remaining 1 tablespoon oil to the pot. Add the onions and bell pepper and sauté, stirring, until the onions are translucent, 3–4 minutes. Return the fish and juices to the pot and add the tomatoes, bouquet garni, basil, ground pepper and the remaining stock. Cover and simmer gently over very low heat until the fish flakes when pierced with a fork and is opaque throughout, about 15 minutes. The stew will form more liquid as it cooks.

Remove from the heat and add the green and black olives, stirring them in gently. Let stand, covered, for 5 minutes. Remove the bouquet garni and discard.

Spoon into warmed bowls and serve.

Serves 4

Saffron Fish Stew

2 tablespoons olive oil

2 cloves garlic, finely chopped

2 sweet onions, cut in half lengthwise
and then crosswise into slices ½ inch
(12 mm) thick

3 shallots, finely chopped

1 large celery stalk, sliced crosswise
into pieces ¼ inch (6 mm) thick

4 white boiling potatoes, peeled and
cut into 1-inch (2.5-cm) cubes

1 cup (8 oz/250 ml) fish stock
(recipe on page 8)

¼ cup (2 fl oz/60 ml) dry white wine

¼ teaspoon crumbled saffron threads

bouquet garni *(recipe on page 10)*

4 lemon zest strips, each about ¼ inch
(6 mm) wide and 3 inches (7.5 cm)
long

2 teaspoons dried herbes de Provence

1½ lb (750 g) assorted white fish fillets,
such as cod, red snapper or flounder,
each ½–¾ inch (12 mm–2 cm) thick,
cut into pieces 2 by 3 inches
(5 by 7.5 cm)

salt and freshly ground pepper

Saffron adds subtle bitterness and beautiful color to this dish. Serve over slices of French bread that have been spread with garlic butter and toasted or grilled.

※

In a 4-qt (4-l) heavy-bottomed stew pot over medium heat, warm the olive oil. Add the garlic, onions, shallots and celery and sauté, stirring, until the onions are translucent, about 8 minutes.

Add the potatoes, fish stock, wine, saffron, bouquet garni, lemon zest and herbes de Provence. Stir well and bring to a low boil over medium heat. Reduce the heat to medium-low, cover and simmer for 15 minutes, to blend the flavors.

Add the fish pieces, gently pushing them down into the liquid so they are fully immersed. Reduce the heat to low, cover and simmer gently until the fish flakes when pierced with a fork and is opaque throughout, 10–15 minutes. Remove the bouquet garni and discard. Season to taste with salt and pepper.

Spoon into warmed bowls and serve.

Serves 4

Fish Stew with Chinese Radish

1 tablespoon vegetable oil

1 cup (8 oz/250 g) peeled and grated mild Chinese radish (lo bok)

3 firm white boiling potatoes, peeled and cut lengthwise into strips about 2½ inches (6 cm) long and ½ inch (12 mm) thick

2 small zucchini (courgettes), cut crosswise into slices ¼ inch (6 mm) thick

1½ cups (12 fl oz/375 ml) fish stock (*recipe on page 8*)

2 lb (1 kg) cod fillets, each ½–¾ inch (12 mm–2 cm) thick, cut crosswise into strips 1½ inches (4 cm) wide

1 tablespoon finely chopped fresh tarragon or 1½ teaspoons dried tarragon

1 large yellow bell pepper (capsicum), seeded, deribbed and cut lengthwise into strips ½ inch (12 mm) wide

salt and freshly ground pepper

Any flaky white fish, such as sea bass, flounder or sole, will work well in this recipe. If you can't find Chinese radish, substitute any sweet, mild radish variety. For a more substantial meal, serve the stew on a bed of Chinese egg noodles or brown rice.

※

*I*n a 4-qt (4-l) heavy-bottomed stew pot over medium heat, warm the vegetable oil. Add the Chinese radish, potatoes and zucchini and sauté, stirring gently, until the zucchini has begun to soften slightly but is not browned, about 5 minutes.

Add the fish stock and bring to a simmer. Reduce the heat to medium-low, cover and simmer just until the vegetables are tender-crisp, about 10 minutes.

Lay the fish pieces over the vegetables; do not stir them in. Sprinkle with the tarragon and then scatter the bell pepper strips over the top. Cover and simmer gently over low heat until the fish is opaque throughout and flakes easily when pierced with a fork, 10–15 minutes; do not allow the mixture to boil at any time. Season to taste with salt and pepper.

Spoon into warmed bowls and serve.

Serves 4

Tuna with Lemongrass

2 tablespoons vegetable oil

1 piece dried red chili pepper, about
½ inch (12 mm) long

1 lb (500 g) tuna fillets, each ¾–1 inch
(2–2.5 cm) thick, cut into 1½-inch
(4-cm) pieces

1 clove garlic, finely chopped

1½ cups (12 fl oz/375 ml) fish stock
(recipe on page 8)

1 small yellow summer squash, cut on
the diagonal into slices ½ inch
(12 mm) thick

1 lemongrass stalk, trimmed, cut in half
lengthwise and then cut crosswise into
3-inch (7.5-cm) lengths and separated

1 red bell pepper (capsicum), seeded,
deribbed and cut lengthwise into
strips ½ inch (12 mm) wide

1 green bell pepper (capsicum), seeded,
deribbed and cut lengthwise into
strips ½ inch (12 mm) wide

2 cups (9 oz/280 g) cauliflower florets

¼ teaspoon ground turmeric

2 green (spring) onions, white part
only, thinly sliced

1 can (8 oz/250 g) baby corn, drained

salt and freshly ground pepper

This dish was inspired by the cuisine of Thailand. Look for lemongrass in Asian food shops and the vegetable section of well-stocked food stores. You may substitute any firm fish fillets for the tuna. Serve over steamed white rice or bean thread noodles.

❋

*I*n a 4-qt (4-l) heavy-bottomed stew pot over medium-high heat, warm the vegetable oil. Add the chili pepper and sauté, stirring, for 1 minute; discard the chili pepper. Add the tuna pieces and garlic to the pot and sauté, stirring, over medium-high heat until the tuna is lightly golden, 2–3 minutes. Using a slotted spoon, transfer the tuna to a dish.

Add the fish stock, squash, lemongrass, red and green bell peppers, cauliflower and turmeric to the pot. Stir gently to mix and bring to a simmer. Reduce the heat to medium-low, cover and simmer gently until the squash is tender-crisp when pierced with a fork, 5–8 minutes.

Return the tuna to the pot and add the green onions and baby corn. Stir gently, cover and continue to simmer gently until the tuna flakes when pierced with a fork and is opaque throughout, about 5 minutes longer. Season to taste with salt and pepper.

Spoon into warmed bowls and serve.

Serves 4

Shrimp and Feta Cheese with Dill

2 tablespoons olive oil

2 large sweet onions, cut into slices ¼ inch (6 mm) thick

2 cloves garlic, minced

1 green bell pepper (capsicum), seeded, deribbed and cut lengthwise into strips ½ inch (12 mm) wide

1 cup (8 fl oz/250 ml) fish stock (*recipe on page 8*)

1 can (28 oz/875 g) whole tomatoes in purée, with juices

4 tablespoons finely chopped fresh dill

½ lb (250 g) feta cheese, crumbled

¼–½ teaspoon freshly ground pepper

1 lb (500 g) shrimp (prawns), peeled and deveined (*see glossary, page 107*)

salt, optional

The feta cheese adds a slight tang to this beautiful dish. Do not be tempted to substitute dried dill for the fresh herb; the resulting taste will be lacking. Serve the stew spooned over orzo garnished with a sprig of fresh dill.

※

*I*n a 4-qt (4-l) heavy-bottomed stew pot over medium heat, warm the olive oil. Add the onions, garlic and bell pepper and sauté, stirring, just until the vegetables start to turn golden, 5–8 minutes. Add the fish stock, tomatoes and juices and dill. Stir well and bring to a simmer. Reduce the heat to medium-low, cover and simmer gently until the vegetables are soft and the stew has thickened slightly, about 20 minutes.

Add the feta cheese, ground pepper and shrimp, pushing the shrimp down into the liquid so they are fully immersed. Bring to a simmer over medium-low heat, cover and simmer gently until the shrimp turn pink and curl, about 8 minutes. Do not overcook the shrimp or they will be tough. Remove from the heat and stir gently. Season with salt, if necessary.

Spoon into warmed shallow bowls or plates and serve.

Serves 4

Halibut with Ginger and Onions

¼ cup (2 oz/60 g) butter or margarine
2 shallots, finely chopped
4 sweet onions, cut in half lengthwise
and then crosswise into slices ½ inch
(12 mm) thick
1 piece fresh ginger, about 1 inch
(2.5 cm) long, peeled and quartered
lengthwise
4 green (spring) onions, including
tender green tops, cut on the diagonal
into 1-inch (2.5-cm) lengths
⅔ cup (5 fl oz/160 ml) fish stock
(*recipe on page 8*)
½ cup (4 fl oz/125 ml) dry white wine
4 halibut or cod steaks, each about
6 oz (185 g) and ¾–1 inch (2–2.5 cm)
thick
salt and freshly ground pepper

Low in fat but packed with flavor, this dish takes only minutes to prepare. Serve over peeled, boiled potatoes and garnish with chopped fresh dill and lemon wedges, if you like.

※

*I*n a 4-qt (4-l) heavy-bottomed stew pot over medium heat, melt the butter or margarine. Add the shallots, sweet onions, ginger and green onions and sauté, stirring, until the onions are translucent, 8–10 minutes.

Add the fish stock and wine, stir well and bring to a simmer. Reduce the heat to medium-low and add the fish, pushing the steaks down into the liquid so they are fully immersed. Cover and simmer gently over medium-low heat until the fish flakes when pierced with a fork and is opaque throughout, 10–15 minutes. Remove the ginger and discard. Season to taste with salt and pepper.

Spoon into warmed shallow bowls and serve.

Serves 4

Scallops and Broccoli

1 tablespoon butter or margarine

1 cup (4 oz/125 g) coarsely chopped
   sweet onion

1 lb (500 g) baby carrots, peeled

3½ cups (10 oz/315 g) broccoli florets,
   including ¾ inch (2 cm) of the stalk

1½ lb (750 g) bay scallops

1½ cups (12 fl oz/375 ml) fish stock
   (recipe on page 8)

2 tablespoons coarsely chopped,
   drained oil-packed sun-dried
   tomatoes

2 teaspoons sake, optional

salt and freshly ground pepper

The small size of bay scallops, usually only about ½ inch (12 mm) in diameter, makes them a nice addition to soups and stews. In this dish, sun-dried tomatoes and the Chinese rice wine known as sake add a pleasantly sharp bite. You can use purchased fish stock in place of the homemade; if you do, you may need to reduce the sun-dried tomato to 1 tablespoon to compensate for the greater saltiness of the store-bought ingredient.

※

*I*n a 4-qt (4-l) heavy-bottomed stew pot over medium heat, melt the butter or margarine. Add the onion and carrots and sauté, stirring, until the carrots are slightly tender and the onion is translucent, about 8 minutes.

Add the broccoli and scallops and stir gently to mix well. Add the fish stock and sun-dried tomatoes. Bring to a simmer but do not allow the mixture to boil. Reduce the heat to low, cover and simmer very gently until the scallops are tender and just opaque in the center, 6–8 minutes. Do not overcook the scallops or they will be tough. Stir in the sake, if using. Season to taste with salt and pepper.

Spoon into warmed bowls and serve.

Serves 6

Shrimp Creole

2 slices bacon or 2 tablespoons butter or margarine
2 celery stalks, finely chopped
2 sweet onions, coarsely chopped
2 green bell peppers (capsicums), seeded, deribbed and coarsely chopped
1 can (28 oz/875 g) whole tomatoes in purée, with juices
4 or more dashes hot-pepper sauce, such as Tabasco
1 lb (500 g) small shrimp (prawns), peeled and deveined (*see glossary, page 107*)
freshly ground pepper

To reduce the calories in this updated version of a Louisiana standard, omit the bacon and use the butter or margarine instead. The result will still be delectable. Steamed white rice is a natural accompaniment.

❋

*I*f using the bacon, in a 4-qt (4-l) heavy-bottomed stew pot over medium heat, fry it until crisp. Using a slotted spoon or tongs, transfer the bacon to paper towels to drain, reserving the drippings in the pot. When cool enough to handle, crumble the bacon; set aside. If using butter or margarine, melt it in the pot over medium heat.

Add the celery, onions and bell peppers to the pot and sauté, stirring, over medium heat until the onions are translucent, about 5 minutes. Add the tomatoes and juices and the hot-pepper sauce. Stir well and bring to a simmer. Reduce the heat to medium-low, cover and simmer until the vegetables are tender and the stew has thickened, about 20 minutes.

Add the shrimp, pushing them down into the liquid so they are fully immersed. Simmer gently, uncovered, over medium-low heat just until the shrimp turn pink and curl, 5–8 minutes. Do not overcook the shrimp or they will be tough. Season to taste with pepper.

To serve, spoon into warmed shallow bowls or plates and garnish with the reserved bacon, if using. Serve immediately.

Serves 4

Salmon and Pesto with Rice

2 tablespoons pine nuts

1½ lb (750 g) salmon fillets, each about ½ inch (12 mm) thick, cut into 1-inch (2.5-cm) pieces

⅓ cup (3 oz/90 g) store-bought pesto

2 tablespoons butter or margarine

2 shallots, finely chopped

1 lb (500 g) small white boiling onions, peeled (see glossary, page 106) and quartered

1 cup (7 oz/220 g) long-grain white rice

2½ cups (20 fl oz/625 ml) fish stock (recipe on page 8)

⅔ cup (5 fl oz/160 ml) dry white wine

1 lb (500 g) cherry tomatoes, halved

salt and freshly ground pepper

Store-bought pesto sauce makes this one-pot stew, with its striking colors, a snap to prepare. Look for deep red salmon fillets to give sharp contrast to this dish. Serve with slices of toasted garlic bread and garnish with fresh basil sprigs.

✳

*P*reheat an oven to 350°F (180°C). Spread the pine nuts on a baking sheet and bake, stirring occasionally, until lightly toasted, 3–5 minutes. Set aside.

In a bowl, toss together the salmon and pesto, coating the fish evenly. Set aside.

In a 4-qt (4-l) heavy-bottomed stew pot over medium heat, melt the butter or margarine. Add the shallots and onions and sauté, stirring, until the shallots are translucent, about 5 minutes. Add the rice, fish stock and wine and stir well. Bring to a simmer. Reduce the heat to medium-low, cover and simmer gently for 15 minutes.

Spread the pesto-coated salmon and the tomatoes evenly over the rice without stirring. Cover and cook over low heat until the rice is tender and the salmon is cooked through, 25–30 minutes. Season to taste with salt and pepper.

To serve, spoon into warmed shallow bowls and sprinkle with the toasted pine nuts. Serve immediately.

Serves 4–6

Curried Lobster Stew

2 tablespoons butter or margarine
1 large sweet onion, coarsely chopped
1 green bell pepper (capsicum), seeded,
    deribbed and coarsely chopped
1 McIntosh or other sweet red apple,
    peeled, quartered, cored and coarsely
    chopped
1 teaspoon curry powder
1 tomato, seeded and coarsely chopped
1 cup (8 fl oz/250 ml) fish stock
    (recipe on page 8)
½ teaspoon ground ginger
¾ lb (375 g) cooked lobster meat,
    picked over for shell fragments, cut
    into 1-inch (2.5-cm) pieces
salt and freshly ground pepper

This special-occasion dish is also delicious made with cooked crab meat. Do not settle for imitation crab meat (surimi) for this preparation or its special character will be lost. Serve atop a bed of wild rice, if you like.

※

*I*n a 4-qt (4-l) heavy-bottomed stew pot over medium heat, melt the butter or margarine. Add the onion, bell pepper, apple and curry powder and sauté, stirring, until the vegetables are tender-crisp, about 5 minutes. Add the tomato, fish stock and ginger. Stir well and bring to a simmer. Reduce the heat to medium-low, cover and simmer gently until thickened and the vegetables are very tender, about 20 minutes.

Stir in the lobster meat and continue to simmer gently, uncovered, over medium-low heat, until the lobster is heated through, about 5 minutes. Do not overcook the lobster or it will be tough. Season to taste with salt and pepper.

Spoon into warmed shallow bowls or plates and serve.

Serves 4

Cabbage Stuffed with Brown Rice in Tomato Sauce

1 head green cabbage, placed in the freezer overnight, then thawed at room temperature

FOR THE FILLING:
2 cups (10 oz/315 g) cooled, cooked brown rice
1 egg, beaten
1 cup (6 oz/185 g) golden raisins (sultanas)
½ cup (2 oz/60 g) chopped walnuts
¼ teaspoon freshly ground pepper
½ cup (2½ oz/75 g) finely chopped yellow onion
½ teaspoon salt

FOR THE SAUCE:
2 tablespoons olive oil
2 sweet onions, coarsely chopped
2 cloves garlic, finely chopped
1 can (28 oz/875 g) whole tomatoes in purée, with juices
1 cup (8 fl oz/250 ml) vegetable stock (*recipe on page 8*)
2 tablespoons brown sugar
1 tablespoon fresh lemon juice

salt and freshly ground pepper

This version of traditional baked cabbage is made easier by eliminating the blanching of the cabbage leaves. Instead, the leaves are frozen and then defrosted, which wilts them so they can be rolled easily. For an interesting variation, add 1 teaspoon caraway seeds to the sauce.

Using a small, sharp knife, cut out the core from the base of the cabbage. Separate the leaves from the cabbage head and set aside.

To make the filling, in a bowl, combine the rice, egg, raisins, walnuts, pepper, onion and salt. Mix well. Place about ¼ cup (1½ oz/45 g) of the filling in the bottom center of each leaf, fold in the sides of the leaf and then roll up the leaf tightly. Set the stuffed leaves aside, seam side down.

To make the sauce, in an 8-qt (8-l) heavy-bottomed stew pot over medium heat, warm the olive oil. Add the onions and garlic and sauté, stirring, until the onions are soft, about 10 minutes. Add the tomatoes and juices, vegetable stock, sugar and lemon juice and stir well.

Carefully add the stuffed cabbage leaves to the sauce, seam sides down. Reduce the heat to low, cover and simmer very gently until the cabbage is cooked and the flavors are blended, about 40 minutes. Do not allow the sauce to boil or the cabbage rolls may break apart. Season to taste with salt and pepper.

To serve, using a large serving spoon, carefully transfer the cabbage rolls to warmed shallow bowls and spoon the sauce over the top.

Makes about 12 cabbage rolls; serves 6

Chili with Cornmeal Dumplings

2 teaspoons olive oil

2 green bell peppers (capsicums), seeded, deribbed and cut lengthwise into strips ½ inch (12 mm) wide

1 large sweet onion, cut in half and then into slices ½ inch (12 mm) thick

2 cans (19 oz/590 g each) red kidney beans, with liquid

2 cups (12 oz/375 g) canned tomato chunks in purée, with juices

1 tablespoon chili powder

3–5 dashes hot-pepper sauce, such as Tabasco

salt and freshly ground pepper

cornmeal dumplings (recipe on page 13)

1 cup (4 oz/125 g) grated Colby or Monterey jack cheese, optional

2 tablespoons chopped fresh cilantro (fresh coriander)

You can garnish this hearty one-dish vegetarian meal with sour cream or plain low-fat yogurt in place of the cheese.

In an 8-qt (8-l) heavy-bottomed stew pot over medium-high heat, warm the olive oil. Add the bell peppers and onion and sauté, stirring, until the onion is translucent, about 5 minutes. Add the kidney beans and their liquid, tomatoes and their juices, chili powder and hot-pepper sauce. Mix well and bring to a simmer. Reduce the heat to medium-low, cover and simmer gently for 20 minutes. Season to taste with salt and pepper.

Add the cornmeal dumplings to the top of the stew, cover and cook as directed.

To serve, spoon the stew and dumplings into warmed bowls and sprinkle with the cheese, if using, and cilantro.

Serves 6

Chick-peas with Zucchini and Tomatoes

2 tablespoons olive oil

2 cloves garlic, minced

1 large sweet onion, cut into wedges ½ inch (12 mm) thick

2 zucchini (courgettes), cut crosswise into slices ½ inch (12 mm) thick

1 red bell pepper (capsicum), seeded, deribbed and cut lengthwise into strips ½ inch (12 mm) wide

1 lb (500 g) cherry tomatoes

½ cup (4 fl oz/125 ml) dry red wine

1½ cups (12 oz/375 g) canned tomato chunks in purée, with juices

1 can (20 oz/625 g) chick-peas (garbanzo beans), drained

½ teaspoon dried oregano

½ teaspoon dried basil

salt and freshly ground pepper

You can use 1 cup (8 oz/250 g) dried chick-peas in place of the canned. Soak the dried chick-peas for 3 hours in water to cover, then drain and proceed as directed in the recipe, increasing the cooking time to cook the chick-peas until tender, about 1 hour. Offer toasted pita bread triangles alongside.

In a 4-qt (4-l) heavy-bottomed stew pot over medium heat, warm the olive oil. Add the garlic, onion and zucchini and sauté, stirring, until the onion is translucent, about 10 minutes. Add the bell pepper, cherry tomatoes, wine, canned tomatoes and juices, chick-peas, oregano and basil. Stir well and bring to a simmer. Reduce the heat to medium-low, cover and simmer gently until the stew is slightly thickened and the vegetables are tender, about 25 minutes. Season to taste with salt and pepper.

Spoon into warmed shallow bowls or plates and serve.

Serves 4

Stuffed Grape Leaves

1 jar (8 oz/250 g) grape leaves, drained

FOR THE FILLING:
1 tablespoon olive oil
1 cup (5 oz/155 g) yellow onion, finely chopped
2 cloves garlic, finely chopped
½ cup (2½ oz/75 g) pine nuts
½ cup (2½ oz/75 g) finely chopped pitted green olives
2 cups (10 oz/315 g) cooled, cooked white rice
salt and freshly ground pepper

FOR THE SAUCE:
2 tablespoons butter or margarine
2 tablespoons all-purpose (plain) flour
1½ cups (12 fl oz/375 ml) vegetable or chicken stock (*recipes on pages 8–9*)
1 tablespoon fresh lemon juice
1 cup (8 oz/250 g) plain yogurt
salt and freshly ground pepper
2 tablespoons finely chopped fresh mint

These popular rice-stuffed grape leaves, known as dolmas, can be served hot or at room temperature. Accompany with sliced cucumbers tossed with plain yogurt, mint and freshly ground pepper.

Rinse the grape leaves in cool water and pat dry with paper towels. Set aside.

In a 4-qt (4-l) heavy-bottomed stew pot over medium heat, warm the olive oil. Add the onion and garlic and sauté, stirring, until the onion is translucent, about 5 minutes. Remove from the heat and add the pine nuts, olives, rice and salt and pepper to taste. Mix well.

Place each grape leaf, shiny side down, on a work surface and place 1 rounded tablespoonful of the filling in the bottom center. Fold the sides of each leaf inward over the filling and then roll up tightly. Set aside, seam side down.

To make the sauce, in a 4-qt (4-l) heavy-bottomed stew pot over medium heat, melt the butter or margarine. Whisk in the flour and cook, whisking constantly, for 2–3 minutes; do not brown. Slowly whisk in the stock and stir until smooth and slightly thickened, 2–3 minutes. Whisk in the lemon juice.

Carefully place the stuffed grape leaves, seam side down, in the pot, layering them if necessary. Cover and cook over medium-low heat until the sauce has thickened and the flavors have blended, about 45 minutes; do not allow to boil.

Using a slotted spoon, transfer the stuffed leaves to a serving platter or individual plates. Reduce the heat to very low and whisk in the yogurt. Do not allow the sauce to boil or it may separate. Season to taste with salt and pepper. Spoon the sauce over the stuffed grape leaves and garnish with the mint.

Makes about 25 stuffed grape leaves; serves 4–6 as a main dish

Lima Beans with Vegetables

1 cup (7 oz/220 g) dried lima beans

2 tablespoons olive oil

1 large sweet onion, cut into 1-inch (2.5-cm) pieces

3 carrots, peeled and cut into 1-inch (2.5-cm) pieces

2 celery stalks, coarsely chopped

1 cup (8 fl oz/250 ml) vegetable stock (*recipe on page 8*)

bouquet garni (*recipe on page 10*)

2 tomatoes, cut into ¾-inch (2-cm) wedges

salt and freshly ground pepper

Bulgur or kasha is a wonderful accompaniment to this savory vegetable stew. If you like, garnish it with garlic-flavored croutons or toasted sesame seeds. You can reconstitute dried lima beans by letting them soak as directed in the recipe or by using the quick-soak method: Place the beans in a 2-qt (2-l) pan and add 4 cups (32 fl oz/1 l) water, or to cover. Set over high heat and bring to a boil. Boil for 2 minutes, remove from the heat and set aside for 1 hour, then drain and rinse before using.

※

Pick over and discard any damaged beans or stones. Rinse the beans. Place in a bowl, add plenty of water to cover and let stand for at least 4 hours or overnight. Drain the lima beans, rinse and set aside.

In a 4-qt (4-l) heavy-bottomed stew pot over medium heat, warm the olive oil. Add the onion, carrots and celery and sauté, stirring, until the vegetables just start to turn golden, about 10 minutes. Add the vegetable stock and, using a large spoon, deglaze the pot over medium-high heat by stirring to dislodge any browned bits from the pot bottom. Add the bouquet garni, the reserved lima beans and tomatoes. Stir well and bring to a simmer. Reduce the heat to medium-low, cover and simmer gently until the carrots are tender and the liquid has thickened slightly, about 20 minutes. Remove the bouquet garni and discard. Season to taste with salt and pepper.

Spoon into warmed shallow bowls or plates and serve.

Serves 4

Italian Green Beans with Cannellini Beans

1 lb (500 g) small white or yellow boiling onions

2 tablespoons olive oil

1 yellow onion, coarsely chopped

2 cloves garlic, finely chopped

1 lb (500 g) Italian (romano) green beans, ends trimmed and cut on the diagonal into 2-inch (5-cm) lengths

4 long Italian green sweet peppers (capsicums), seeded, deribbed and cut lengthwise into strips ½ inch (12 mm) wide

1 can (20 oz/625 g) cannellini, Great Northern or white kidney beans, drained

6 large plum (Roma) tomatoes, cut crosswise into quarters

½ cup (2½ oz/75 g) pitted small black olives

1 tablespoon fresh oregano leaves or 1 teaspoon dried oregano

1 tablespoon thinly sliced fresh basil or 1 teaspoon dried basil

salt and freshly ground pepper

The canned white beans make this an especially quick recipe to prepare. If you can't find the long Italian sweet peppers, use green bell peppers instead. Serve this savory ragout over bowls of creamy polenta or cooked linguine and garnish with fresh oregano or basil sprigs.

Using a sharp knife, trim off the root ends of the boiling onions. Cut a shallow X in each trimmed end (to keep the onions whole during cooking). In a pot, combine the onions with plenty of water to cover. Bring to a boil. Boil for about 2 minutes. Drain and, when cool enough to handle, slip off the skins. Set the onions aside.

In a 4-qt (4-l) heavy-bottomed stew pot over medium heat, warm the olive oil. Add the chopped onion and garlic and sauté, stirring, until the onion is translucent, about 5 minutes. Add the green beans, sweet peppers and the reserved boiling onions. Continue to sauté until the peppers just start to soften, about 5 minutes longer.

Add the cannellini, Great Northern or white kidney beans; tomatoes; olives; oregano and basil. Cover and cook over medium-low heat until the green beans are tender, about 15 minutes. Season to taste with salt and pepper.

Spoon into warmed shallow bowls and serve.

Serves 4–6

Glossary

The following glossary defines terms both generally and specifically as they relate to stews and their preparation. Included are major and unusual ingredients and basic preparation techniques.

BEAN THREAD NOODLES
Thin, transparent noodles made from mung bean starch in China and potato starch in Japan. Also known as silver noodles, cellophane noodles and transparent noodles.

BELGIAN ENDIVE
Leaf vegetable with refreshing, slightly bitter spear-shaped leaves, white to pale yellow-green—or sometimes red—in color and tightly packed in cylindrical heads 4–6 inches (10–15 cm) long. Also known as chicory or witloof.

BELL PEPPERS
Sweet-fleshed, bell-shaped member of the pepper family. Also known as capsicum. Most common in the unripe green form, although ripened red or yellow varieties are also available. Long Italian sweet peppers are slightly sweeter and more slender than regular peppers.

BUTTERNUT SQUASH
A pale yellowish tan winter squash with yellow to orange flesh. Commonly about 8–12 inches (20–30 cm) long, with a broad bulblike base and a more slender neck.

CABBAGE, CHINESE
Asian variety of cabbage with long, mild-flavored pale green to white, crisp leaves. Also known as napa cabbage or celery cabbage.

CARAWAY SEEDS
Small, crescent-shaped dried seeds used whole or ground as a popular savory seasoning.

CAYENNE PEPPER
Very hot ground spice derived from dried cayenne chili peppers.

CHILI SEASONINGS
Many forms of dried red chili peppers may be used to add their subtle or strong flavors to stews. Among the most common, included in this book, are:

Chili Powder
Commercial blend of spices featuring ground dried chili peppers along with such other seasonings as cumin, oregano, cloves, coriander, pepper and salt. Best purchased in small quantities, as flavor diminishes rapidly after opening.

Chili Sauce
Commercial bottled blend of hot and mild chili peppers, vinegar, sugar and other flavorings. Some varieties are also tomato-based. Use as a seasoning ingredient or a condiment.

Dried Red Chilies
A wide variety of red chili pods can be dried and added to stews, either whole or crumbled. For the recipes found here, use dried jalapeños or traditional small red chilies. Found in Asian or Latin American markets and well-stocked food stores.

Ground Dried Chili
Pure ground dried chili peppers, ranging in strength from mild to hot depending upon chili variety used. Available in spice sections and ethnic food sections of food stores, as well as in Latin American and Asian markets.

CHINESE FIVE-SPICE POWDER
Popular ground savory seasoning, reddish brown in color, usually combining star anise, fennel or aniseeds, cloves, cinnamon and Sichuan peppercorns. Sold in Asian markets and in ethnic food sections of food stores.

CILANTRO
Green, leafy herb resembling flat-leaf (Italian) **parsley,** with a sharp, aromatic, somewhat astringent flavor. Popular in Latin American and Asian cuisines. Also called fresh coriander and commonly referred to as Chinese parsley.

BEANS
All kinds of canned or dried beans and peas may be used as an ingredient in stews. Dried beans should be carefully picked over to remove any impurities, such as small stones or fibers, or any discolored or misshapen beans. Next, to rehydrate them, whole dried beans are often presoaked in cold water to cover generously for a few hours. In the case of shorter-cooking stews, already cooked canned beans or fresh green beans may also be used.

Some of the more common bean varieties used in stews in this book include:

Cannellini Beans
Italian variety of small, white, thin-skinned oval beans. Great Northern or white (navy) beans may be substituted.

Chick-peas
Round, tan member of the pea family (below), with a slightly crunchy texture and nutlike flavor. Also known as garbanzo beans or ceci beans.

Kidney Beans
Widely popular kidney-shaped beans (below), with brownish red skins, slightly mealy texture and robust flavor. White kidney beans are also available.

Lima Beans
Flat, greenish-white kidney-shaped beans with a mild flavor and soft texture.

Italian Green Beans
Long, flat green beans (below), also known as romano beans. Primarily available fresh, Italian green beans are longer, wider and flatter than most other green bean varieties.

White (Navy) Beans
Small, white, thin-skinned oval beans. Also known as soldier or Boston beans.

CORNISH HEN
Small hybrid bird, also known as rock Cornish game hen, that usually yields a single serving. Although sometimes available fresh, they are most often found in the freezer section of food markets.

CORNSTARCH
Fine, powdery flour ground from the endosperm of corn—the white heart of the kernel—and used as a neutral-flavored thickening agent in some stews. Also known as cornflour.

CURRY POWDER
Generic term for blends of spices commonly used to flavor East Indian–style dishes. Most curry powders will include coriander, cumin, **ground dried chili**, fenugreek and **turmeric**; other additions may include cardamom, cinnamon, cloves, allspice, fennel seeds and **ginger**. Best purchased in small quantities, because flavor diminishes rapidly after opening.

DIJON MUSTARD
Mustard made in Dijon, France, from dark brown mustard seeds (unless otherwise marked *blanc*) and white wine or wine vinegar. Pale in color, fairly hot and sharp tasting, true Dijon mustard and non-French blends labeled "Dijon-style" are widely available in food stores.

FETA CHEESE
White cheese made from sheep's or goat's milk, notable for its salty, sharp flavor and crumbly interior and a consistency that ranges from creamy to dry.

GRAPE LEAVES
In Greek and other Middle Eastern cuisines, grapevine leaves (above, right) are commonly used as edible wrappers. If fresh leaves are available, rinse them thoroughly before use. Bottled leaves, available in ethnic delicatessens and the specialty-food section of well-stocked food markets, should be gently rinsed of their brine before use.

HERBES DE PROVENCE
A commercially sold dried herb blend typical of the Provence region of south central France; it may include rosemary, **thyme**, savory and such other local seasonings as oregano, basil and lavender blossoms.

HOT-PEPPER SAUCE
Bottled commercial cooking and table sauce made from fresh or hot **dried red chilies**. Many varieties are available, but Tabasco is the most commonly known brand.

GINGER
The rhizome of the tropical ginger plant, which yields a sweet, strong-flavored spice. Whole ginger rhizomes (below), commonly but mistakenly called roots, may be purchased fresh in most markets. Ground, dried ginger can be found in jars or tins in the spice section.

JUNIPER BERRIES
Small, dried aromatic berries of the juniper tree. Available in the spice section of well-stocked food stores.

KALE
Member of the cabbage family (below), with long, dark green, crinkly leaves that have a strong taste and fairly sturdy texture—characteristics that suit them well to the long, slow simmering of a stew.

LEEKS
Sweet, moderately flavored member of the onion family, long and cylindrical in shape with a pale white root end and dark green leaves. Grown in sandy soil, the leafy-topped, multilayered vegetables require thorough cleaning.

LEMONGRASS
Thick, stalklike grass with a sharp, lemony flavor; popular in Southeast Asian cooking and available fresh or dried in some Asian food stores. If fresh lemongrass is unavailable, substitute 1 tablespoon dried lemongrass for each 8-inch (20-cm) stalk of fresh; or substitute long, thin strips of lemon peel.

MANGO
Tropical fruit with juicy, aromatic orange flesh. Ripe mangoes yield slightly to finger pressure; ripen firm mangoes at room temperature in an open paper or plastic bag. The skin peels easily when slit with a knife. Slice the flesh from both sides of the large, flat pit, as well as from around its edges.

MARSALA
Dry or sweet amber Italian wine from the area of Marsala, in Sicily.

MOLASSES
Thick, robust-tasting, syrupy sugarcane by-product of sugar refining. Light (unsulfured) molasses results from the first boiling of the syrup; dark molasses from the second boiling.

MUSHROOMS
With their meaty textures and rich, earthy flavors, mushrooms are used to enrich many stews. Cultivated white mushrooms (right) are widely available in food markets and greengrocers; in their smallest form, with their caps still closed, they are often descriptively called button mushrooms. Straw mushrooms (below) are a small, plump, brown variety resembling closed umbrellas, named for the beds of straw on which they grow in China. The canned variety, most often used, is available in well-stocked food stores.

OKRA
Small, mild, slender green vegetable pods, 1½–3 inches (4–7.5 cm) in length, with crisp outer flesh and thick, mucilaginous juices when cooked.

OLIVES
Good-quality cured black olives, such as French Niçoise, Greek Kalamata or Italian Gaeta varieties, are sold in well-stocked food stores. Green olives are sometimes preferred for their sharper flavor.

GLOSSARY

ORZO
Small, rice-shaped pasta.

PAPAYA
Tropical fruit shaped somewhat like a large pear or avocado, with soft, sweet orange flesh—milder tasting than a **mango**—and smooth yellow skin when ripe. Halve lengthwise and scoop out the shiny black seeds before peeling.

PAPRIKA
Powdered spice derived from the dried paprika pepper; popular in several European cuisines and available in sweet, mild and hot forms. Hungarian paprika is the best, but Spanish paprika, which is mild, may also be used. Buy in small quantities from shops with a high turnover, to ensure a fresh, flavorful supply.

PARSLEY
This widely used fresh herb is available in two varieties: the more popular curly-leaf type and a flat-leaf type, also known as Italian parsley (shown here).

PARSNIP
Root vegetable similar in shape and texture to the carrot, but with ivory flesh and an appealingly sweet flavor.

PEPPERCORNS
Pepper, the most common of all savory spices, is best purchased as whole peppercorns, to be ground in a pepper mill as needed, or coarsely crushed. Pungent black peppercorns derive from slightly underripe pepper berries, whose hulls oxidize as they dry. Milder white peppercorns come from fully ripened berries, with the husks removed before drying. Sharp-tasting unripened green peppercorns are sold water-packed, pickled in brine or dried. Rinse brine-packed peppercorns before using.

PESTO
Traditional Milanese sauce made of puréed basil, garlic, **pine nuts,** Parmesan cheese and olive oil; traditionally tossed with pasta and sometimes used as a seasoning for stews and other dishes. Ready-made pesto can be found in the refrigerated section of well-stocked food stores.

PINE NUTS
Small, ivory-colored seeds extracted from the cones of a species of pine tree, with a rich, slightly resinous flavor. Used whole as an ingredient or garnish.

POTATOES
While the kinds of potatoes and the names they go by vary from region to region, some common varieties include:

Baking potatoes
Large potatoes with thick brown skins that have a dry, mealy texture when cooked. Also known as russet or Idaho potatoes.

White boiling potatoes
Medium-sized potatoes with thin tan skins. When cooked, their textures are finer than baking potatoes but coarser than yellow-tinged waxy varieties.

New potatoes
New potatoes are any variety of potato harvested in early summer when small and immature. As a result, their flesh is sweeter and more tender. Most are red-skinned, although yellow-skinned new potatoes can also be found.

Sweet potatoes
Not true potatoes, although resembling them in form, these tuberous vegetables have light to deep red skin and pale yellow to orange flesh prized for its sweetness when cooked. The light-skinned variety is the most common.

Yam-type sweet potatoes
True yams are large tuberous vegetables native to the Caribbean. Elsewhere, though, the term is sometimes applied to the dark-skinned variety of sweet potato with sweet, deep orange flesh.

ONIONS
All manner of onions are used to enhance the flavor of stews. *Green onions,* also called spring onions or scallions, are a variety harvested immature, leaves and all, before their bulbs have formed. The green and white parts may both be enjoyed, raw or cooked, for their mild but still pronounced onion flavor. *Red (Spanish) onions* are a mild, sweet variety of onion with purplish red skin and red-tinged white flesh. **White-skinned,** *white-fleshed onions* tend to be sweet and mild. *Yellow onions* are the common, white-fleshed, strong-flavored variety distinguished by their dry, yellowish brown skins.

In addition to red (Spanish) onions and some types of white onion, the sweetest U.S. varieties of brown-skinned onions are generally cultivated in and around Walla Walla, Washington; Vidalia, Georgia; and Maui, Hawaii; and they are known and labeled by their place of origin.

Preparing Small Boiling Onions
Small white boiling onions measuring 1½–2 inches (4–5 cm) and pearl onions, measuring ¾–1 inch (2–2.5 cm), are sometimes blanched, then peeled and added whole to stews.

To peel these small onions, trim off the root ends, then cut a shallow X in each trimmed end (so the onion remains whole during cooking). In a pot, combine the pearl onions with plenty of water to cover. Bring to a boil. Boil for about 2 minutes, then drain. When cool enough to handle, slip off the skins by squeezing gently with your fingers.

106

RADISHES, CHINESE AND JAPANESE

Asian varieties of the crisp root vegetable tend to be both larger and milder than most European radishes. Of the Asian radishes, the Chinese radish, also known as lo bok (left), is among the mildest. It is available both light- and dark- skinned, and has a rounded, smooth shape that tapers at the root end. The Japanese daikon (below, right) is slightly more bitter than the Chinese radish, although it is still mild. It has a smooth, light skin and a long, sausagelike shape that can reach up to more than 1 foot (30 cm) in length. Although both may be eaten raw and, like more familiar red radishes, have crisp textures and refreshing flavors characterized by a pungent, peppery hotness, they also stand up well to simmering in stews.

RICE

Rice provides a fitting accompaniment to many stews, and may also be included in some recipes to give a stew more body and texture.

Among the many rice varieties grown, milled and cooked around the world, the most popular type is long-grain white rice, whose slender kernels steam to a light, fluffy consistency. Brown rice is rice from which only the outer husk has been removed during milling, leaving a highly nutritious, fiber-rich coating of bran that gives the grain its distinctive color, chewy texture and nutlike flavor.

SAFFRON

Intensely aromatic, golden orange spice made from the dried stigmas of a species of crocus (below);

used to perfume and color many classic Mediterranean and East Indian dishes. Sold either as threads—the dried stigmas—or in powdered form. Look for products labeled "pure saffron."

SHRIMP

Fresh, raw shrimp (prawns) are generally sold with the heads already removed but the shells still intact. Before cooking they are usually peeled and their thin, vein-like intestinal tracts removed.

Peeling and Deveining

Using your thumbs, split open the shrimp's thin shell along the concave side, between its two rows of legs. Grasp the shell and gently peel it away.

Using a small knife, make a shallow slit along the peeled shrimp's back (see below), just deep enough to expose the long, usually dark, veinlike intestinal tract. With the tip of the knife or your fingers, lift up and pull out the vein, discarding it.

SALT, KOSHER

Coarse-grained salt with no additives and a less salty taste than table salt. Coarse sea salt is an acceptable substitute.

SHALLOT

Small member of the onion family with brown skin, white-to-purple flesh and a flavor resembling a cross between sweet **onion** and garlic.

SHERRY

Fortified, cask-aged wine, ranging from dry to sweet, enjoyed as an aperitif and used as a flavoring in both savory dishes and desserts.

THYME

Fragrant, clean-tasting, small-leaved herb popular fresh or dried as a seasoning for poultry, light meats, seafood or vegetables.

TOMATOES

During summer, when tomatoes are in season, use the best red or yellow sun-ripened tomatoes you can find. At other times of year, plum tomatoes, sometimes called Roma or egg tomatoes, are likely to have the best flavor and texture; for cooking, canned whole plum tomatoes are also good.

Small cherry tomatoes, barely bigger than the fruit after which they are descriptively named, also have a pronounced flavor that makes them ideal candidates for cooking during their peak summer season.

Sun-dried tomatoes (below) have an intense, sweet-tart flavor and a pleasantly chewy texture that enhance savory recipes. Available either dry or packed in oil with or without herbs and spices.

TURMERIC

Pungent, earthy-flavored ground spice that, like **saffron**, adds a vibrant yellow color to any dish.

ZEST

Thin, brightly colored, outermost layer of a citrus fruit's peel, containing most of its aromatic essential oils—a lively source of flavor. Zest may be removed using one of two easy methods:

1. Use a simple tool known as a zester, drawing its sharp-edged holes across the fruit's skin to remove the zest in thin strips. Alternatively, use a fine hand-held grater.

2. Holding the edge of a paring knife or vegetable peeler away from you and almost parallel to the fruit's skin, carefully cut off the zest in thin strips, taking care not to remove any of the bitter white pith with it. Then thinly slice or chop the strips on a cutting board.

Index

ACKNOWLEDGMENTS

The publishers would like to thank the following people and organizations for their generous assistance and support in producing this book:
Sharon C. Lott, Stephen W. Griswold, Patty Draper, Ken DellaPenta, Claire Sanchez, Jim Obata, Jennifer Mullins, the buyers and store managers for Pottery Barn and Williams-Sonoma stores. Special thanks to Lynne Bail for testing all recipes.

The following kindly lent props for the photography: Biordi Art Imports, Candelier, Fillamento, Forrest Jones, Sue Fisher King, RH Shop, and Chuck Williams.